You don't just read a poem by Fran Lock, you become so immersed in it that it becomes the way you think. She has it all: passion; a swift and finely honed intelligence and an intimate knowledge of the weight—the heft and swing —of words. She is the perfect antidote to the dull, insipid nature of so much contemporary literature. Long may she sing.

—Alan Humm

Fiercely intelligent, ideologically rigorous, relentlessly prolific & qualitatively consistent: Fran Lock is a critical but sensitive observer, bearing witness and stripping back the detritus of our lives to a point of revelation. Both intimate & societal relationships are exposed to a thorough & articulate interrogation, wise words & a disciplined rage, spat through a barrage of impassioned spittle. She is a rare & important voice in the contemporary British literary tradition.

—Paul Summers

Fran Lock's poems rasp tender-tenaciously: basking in decaying sun with she and other feral hyena pups, glitter-sand in our fur that's soft and sometimes scabby, is what I want to do.

—Amy Grandvoinet

There are no unnecessary words in Fran Lock's poetry. Political, urban, rural —every line essential. Every image, fabulous.

—Catherine Graham

Fran Lock is our great poet of working-class rage and grief, creating a new language of anger from a bricolage of myth, shapeshifting, alienation, folklore, and moments of hard-won tender wit. Fran's work refuses to go the easy route—it says only what needs to be said, not what poetic fashion requires.

—Nick Moss

Fran Lock's sage poetics are unflinching in erudition for here is a voice for the voiceless, steadfastly calling-out injustices and naming social disparities. This timeless poetry omnibus is, like all Lock's work, an essential and vital elucidation of working-class lives; read these words whilst punching the air with a defiant yes!

—Julie Hogg

There are two characteristics that make Fran Lock's poetry unique. The first is the way in which her writing—always an act of resistance—mirrors the intensity of our beating-down. It's as if she's saying however relentless the assaults of capitalism on our lives and humanity, we will not succumb, we will not go under: we will meet and defeat them. The second is her extraordinary intellectual generosity, the way in which the urgency of her engagement with now is underpinned by the knowledge and sensibility of an historian sage.

—Charlie Hill

Fran Lock's poetry is a persistent rage against the darkness of late capitalism in all its disfigurements. Fiercely working-class, she is a great supporter of the poetry of other poets who are largely ignored by mainstream publishers.

—Peter Raynard

Over the last fifty years I've read literally thousands of poems, I've hosted poetry readings, edited anthologies and written reviews; and in all that time, I've only rarely encountered poetry that makes the hairs on the back of my neck tingle. Fran Lock's work does exactly that. She understands that poetry is a sound as well as a sense. Her poems have the virtue of being completely original, beautifully crafted and above all, they engage the emotions as well as the intellect. She is not some rudderless ship adrift in a sea of vague and ambiguous linguistic possibilities, she has a socialist point of view and that lens brings everything she writes into a razor-sharp focus. She's that comparative rarity, the real thing: a great poet.

—Kevin McCann

Fran's poetry is emotional, dynamic and distinctive and her prose writing is persuasive and clear, both have an undercurrent of intellectual rigour and honesty. She is simply one of the best writers and communicators around today.

—Pauline Sewards

Fran doesn't simply write poetry, she channels it. Her poems are an extraordinary outpouring of acute perception and compassion with a generosity of spirit that knows no bounds.

—Barbara Barnes

Man, it's awkward to write using the same raw materials that Fran Lock uses in order to praise her. Simply, she is the real deal. Cassandra howling into the abyss. I read her poetry with the same awe and wonder that I read the other Romantics, writing 100+ years before her. I think her words will resonate 100+ years hence. She's a wonder, she's a spondee. Worra woman.

—Sarah Barrington

We're somnambulised into expecting poetry to deliver easy comfort or bite-sized 'wisdom' but a Fran Lock poem brings all the visceral shock of cyclone or aria and stops us in our tracks. Fran's words are both weapons and blossoms and each phrase, each image, carries its own febrile charge and posits its own unique world. It's an accumulative rhythmic power that becomes the force of incantation, of rhapsody and prayer. But they're also funny-as-fuck and prise moments of everyday mundanity or madness into their rolling swagger: in short, this is work whose eclecticism and range is captivating and a thing of courageous beauty!

—Al Hutchins

Fran is a magician with words. Mystical yet down to earth. I love how she 'gets' what I try to say. I also laugh out loud at her acute wit. I am grateful to Fran.

—Wendy Young

Fran Lock—visionary, oracle, magician, fury—how is it possible for a poet to hold so much in her extended cry? Reading her is to wonder and weep, and also laugh, revelling in her linguistic joy.

—Sarah Wedderburn

The first time I read Fran Lock's poems I felt like a new world exploded open inside my brain.

—Catherine Ayres

With Fran Lock, it is never just about the poems, stunning, complex, brilliant, vivid with thought, intelligence and power though they are. It is about the never-ending fight to be heard, to be recognised as equal, and Lock will ever stand in solidarity with us. It is about the articulation, using staggering wordsmithery, of our working-class histories, hearts, minds, souls and lived experiences. Lock does this for us with fire, rage, passion and above all, with love for all that we have been, all that we are, and all that we can be.

—Jane Burn

Fran is a generational talent with a stunningly unique and intoxicating vocabulary. She is also a mighty inspiration to those fighting to make poetry be for all, and from all.

—Peadar and Collette O'Donoghue

Sometimes, if we are lucky, we come across creative work that we know immediately is very special: it might be a painting or sculpture, a piece of music, a book, or in the case of Fran Lock, a poem. You will be blown away, entranced and just left buzzing with the intensity and the sheer brilliance of Fran Lock's writing. Her skill with language is positively Shakespearean—it consistently reaches that kind of level of creativity, effectiveness, and a clear understanding of how language can work as much more than just words, just sounds. Fran Lock's writing is of a quality that only comes along very, very rarely—get it while you can.

—Denni Turp

Fran Lock's poetry is much more than insightful, it is psychologically penetrating. She brings to her work a powerful intellect that seeks redress for humanity, and not just social or political redress but ultimately a spiritual one.

—Jim Aitken

Fran Lock is one of my all-time favourite poets. Her writing is verbal fireworks: explosive, subversive, politically charged and shot through with an intelligent spirituality. Everyone should read her!

—Rebecca Lowe

This trilogy is an important retrospective by one of our most original poets —a rich, eloquent, dense and raging book, fierce and wise.

—Andy Croft

Fran Lock is a gift not just to the field of contemporary poetry but also to the poetry community; her generosity towards other poets is as awe-inspiring as her poetic drive and talent. She is more than just a brilliant poet, she is a wonderful human being full of depth, courage, and compassion.

—Golnoosh Nour

Fran Lock is a writer of rare originality, fierce and prolific, an unstoppable tidal wave of a poet, who has formed her own lexicon from myth and language and rage—'my name a subtle heckle on an english tongue'. Every poem of hers is an act of resistance against the false and the fake and the self-satisfied. Her work evokes—or invokes—what we keep, what consoles or taunts us in the dark hours, and offers a vision of 'outsiderhood' as the only way of really belonging to oneself. This language of Fran's is delicate, muscular, expressive and musical. It's the same music as the wind howling in the night, as the muttering of a guy in a doorway, as the roar of a tidal wave—controlled and also free. 'Here are our people, yours and mine', she writes, 'in the grey-pink battery flesh of the poor'.

—Katy Evans-Bush

So much feels flat and lifeless compared to Lock's charged and invigorating language. The poems are alive to the degradation they describe but defiantly without despair... In fact it's closer to the prophetic mode, or the lamentation —with flashes of sublime wordplay and a complexity equal to its unaffected flow. The terrain coolly, precisely observed and vividly pronounced upon. I read these collections for anger, for solidarity, for the white heat of true consolation, but foremost to be reminded of what's possible when real poetry is given the space, intelligence and passion it needs to reach the dormant parts of our brains.

—Luke Kennard

The sheer warp and weft, curl and slap, fork and wind of Fran Lock's poetry gives it a tangibility on the page, a ripeness and sharpness and bittersweetness like grapefruit stinging the tongue. ...A large part of Lock's linguistic genius (and I don't use the latter word lightly) is in so seamlessly merging contemporary and popular-culture images, memes, slang, neologisms and textspeak with a historically literate, nostalgic, hauntological awareness.

—Alan Morrison

Fran's poems don't do received ideas. They bristle with beauty. The work plays out where the broken promises beset us like fucking gnats and shows them up plainly. She goes there because we don't have to... No. We do have to, but she got there first. A proper disrupter of easy lexical credit systems.

—Duncan Jones

Something of the satisfaction of Fran Lock's poetry is in her name. These are poems of resistance against resistance, which turn a tremendous guile and wit on the language of oppression that fathered them. The struggle may be real and ongoing, but these poems take a musical satisfaction in that. Lock understands that doors open when we stop looking for keys.

—Joseph S. Furey, The Times

'There is a magic in the way Fran Lock uses language that makes you feel opened, often astonished, and sometimes even healed. Her writing weaves, dives, dances, hammers itself across the page unlocking all sorts of vaguely felt, but never quite able to be articulated, thoughts and emotions in you. Her writing is like untying a knot that has always nagged at you while stuck in the back of your throat; your mind; your stomach. It startles in its use of language, its hugely entertaining metaphors and its 'fuck what others think' bravery.'

—Martin Hayes

So good to have these three collections of Fran Lock's brilliantly inventive, politically hard-hitting, technically resourceful and—say it!—beautifully crafted poems now brought together in a single volume. Class shows in every sense and in every aspect of this wonderful collection.

—Christopher Norris

/ Spectres
// Defectors
/// No Respecters

A Poetry Omnibus
By Fran Lock

Featuring:

/ Muses & Bruises
// Ruses & Fuses
/// Raptures & Captures

La poesia / non muta nulla. Nulla è sicuro, ma scrivi.
Poetry / changes nothing. Nothing is certain, but write.

—Franco Fortini

First published 2024 by **Culture Matters**.
Culture Matters promotes cultural democracy,
see www.culturematters.org.uk

Edited by Mike Quille
Text © Fran Lock
Images © Fran Lock
Typeset by Alan Morrison
ISBN 978-1-912710-76-8

Acknowledgements

Muses and Bruises—Poems by Fran Lock with collages by Steev Burgess (Culture Matters, 2017); *Ruses and Fuses*—Poems by Fran Lock with collages by Steev Burgess (Culture Matters, 2018); *Raptures and Captures*—Poems by Fran Lock with collages by Steev Burgess (Culture Matters, 2019).

Preface

By Fran Lock

It's hard to believe that it's been nearly ten years since I pitched the first of my weirdly specific ideas for a poetry collection to the then emerging arts and culture cooperative, **Culture Matters**, thus beginning one of the most meaningful and enduring relationships of my writing life so far. **Culture Matters** published that collection, **Muses & Bruises**, and then two follow-up books, **Ruses & Fuses** and **Raptures & Captures**.

Since then, much has changed, for the press, for myself, and for the world. It goes without saying that not all of those changes have been unequivocally positive. We are, it seems, daily inundated by new and previously unimaginable urgencies; the speed and scale at which they unfold demands of us a practically precognitive level of ethical vigilance, fast-mapping webs of interconnected crises in real-time. I was hesitant then, to begin work on this retrospective: would the poems—those early poems in particular—still have anything "relevant" to say?

Then again, relevance is relative. That is, you can't go about declaring relevance (or lack of it) by fiat; what matters and means to historical moments and to individual readers is provisional, subjective, contingent and shifting. Relevance is *not* an inherent or objective *quality*, but a highly politicised *concept*, one that is frequently weaponised by the Right to invalidate Left-leaning causes, and to dismiss the politically charged art produced by Left-wing artists as (at best) anachronistic or (at worst) propagandist ranting.

It could also be argued that it behoves us to resist, where possible, the malignant rapidity of late-stage capitalism, its endless, overwhelming assaults on our time and attention; its hectic, relentless obsession with the cultural zeitgeist, the forced march of the "new". Our rapid-fire news cycle provokes reaction but denies us the space in which to critically engage. Under such conditions concentration and care cannot help but become diffuse and divided. Inside the machine—exhausted and distracted in equal measure—we lose the time to reflect, the opportunity and the energy to meaningfully challenge. This is absolutely tactical. It serves the aims of power.

Muses & Bruises

Poetry, at its best, can make space for the kind of deep, sustained attention seldom afforded to us as citizens or subjects. It can extend this care to those figures and voices not usually honoured within political or cultural traditions; it can allow us—as readers—the room in which our own sorely straitened mental muscles may stretch and breathe. It is the art of *staying with*, of *looking again*.

So, I needn't worry too much about "relevance", I guess. But what am I looking again *at*? What am I making a return *to*? There is an inevitable level of cringe-factor inherent in revisiting prior work, and in so many ways these collections seem to belong—if not to a "simpler time"—to a more optimistic and less tutored poet. On the other hand, the impetus for writing many of these poems remains vitally alive, and in the case of **Muses & Bruises** feels to me more pressing than ever.

Ekphrastic interactions with Greek myth from a feminist perspective are hardly novel. They weren't novel in 2016 either, but in many ways that was the point. In the realm of middle-class literary production, the ekphrastic poem often creates a closed loop of coterie address: an in-joke for those with the benefit of an elite education. In this way, they form a microcosm for wider society. My decision to write about the Mousai was not, in any sense, my begging for admission into that club, but an attempt to trespass and upset its well-maintained borders. My Muses were working-class and Traveller women. They rocked up in the middle of a literary tradition set up to exclude them and they claimed centre stage. It was my way of saying: no, you don't get to keep this to yourselves; these myths and legends can and should belong to everybody.

In the last recorded census, 56.8 per cent of those who identified as Gypsy or Irish Traveller had no qualifications, compared with 18.2 per cent of the population of England and Wales. The suicide rate for Irish Traveller women is six times higher than their settled counterparts. A book of poetry—*any* book of poetry—will never adequately redress this, but it might make a little space, a crack in the carapace of willed inattention. Both the 'Muses' and 'Rag Town Girls' sequences represent my attempts to find a poetic idiom with which to crack that carapace. They're about locating working-class anger within the precincts of a measured, contemplative lyric tradition. They refused to be trapped between the objectifying gaze and annihilating stare of a visual culture, an artistic heritage, and a political reality created and controlled by wealthy men.

Ruses & Fuses

Ruses & Fuses emerged from a different set of considerations. I knew that I wanted to write about English working-class radical histories, but I knew with equal certainty that my own knowledge of those histories was far from complete. So, while **Ruses** is very much about creating an alternative history of radical socialist dissent, it is *also* about the way our knowledge of our own history is distorted and withheld; it is about the often-tangential routes we find into an imaginative community of dissenting others across place and time, and it is about the fragments and ephemera from which any working-class history will inevitably be cobbled.

The poor haunt history—as they haunt civic space—but only the rich live in it. Their posterity is long. They have monuments, architectural and cultural. Buildings, statues, and street names all serve to capture the continuity of *their* lived experience, inscribing memory onto public space. Canonical art archives their histories, museums are full of their things. But posterity is a form of posthumous luxury, thus rarely afforded to the poor. Which is why elites love to talk up the "timelessness" of certain texts; why they invent a metaphysics of inherent value to explain the endurance of their art, and why imperviousness to long attrition is presented as the absolute aim for *all* art and literature. Permanence is not, of course, organic proof of special merit. It is, rather, artificially engineered. And if timelessness is the both the goal and the metric upon which a work will be judged, then the highly specific social conditions under which that art is made can be discounted as merely "topical", of fleeting and limited "relevance". There's that word again.

In both the 'Ruses' and the 'Travesties' sequences, I am thinking about working-class poetry as a form of archival ephemera, as a means of registering presence, as a manically improvised language for social conditions.

This revised and updated version of the text for **Ruses & Fuses** contains several new poems orbiting the figure of Kentish rebel Jack Cade, with whom I have become increasingly obsessed since moving to Kent.

The Jack Cade Rebellion, which took place over the summer months of May, June and July in 1450, was arguably one of the most important popular uprisings to take place in England during the long Middle Ages. It began as an orchestrated demonstration of political unrest by the inhabitants of south-east England (Kent) against the mismanagement and oppression of Henry VI's government. Its participants, both men and women, mostly labourers, artisans, yeomen and farmers expressed concerns over unfair wages and taxes. Their

Bill of Complaint also attacked the cronyism and corruption they perceived at various levels of government and within the church.

The Complaint included an extensive catalogue of judicial misconduct: selling the goods and property of those accused of treason (before they were convicted); leasing of judicial offices to those who used them to gain money through extortion; bringing default judgments against defendants who had been neither summoned nor notified of suits pending against them; and the illegal eviction of people from their property.

While little is known of the historical Jack Cade, we *do* know that his insurrection was popular and initially successful: the Rebellion brought London to a virtual standstill and caused Henry VI to flee the capital for the relative safety of Kenilworth Castle in Warwickshire, some one-hundred miles from the city.

Yet if people have heard of Cade at all, it is usually as an antagonist in Shakespeare's *Henry VI Part II* (first performed in 1592), where his portrayal is complex but not exactly kind. The grievances of the rebels are presented within the play as deeply serious, and would have resonated powerfully with its first audience—by 1570 the purchasing power of agricultural wages was 40 per cent lower than it was in 1450, as a result of which it was nearly impossible to support a household containing young children or infirm adults on wage labour, and by 1592 acts of enclosure had begun to be roundly and publicly condemned.

However, Cade's revolutionary message is continually undercut by his presentation as politically crude, megalomaniacal and bloodthirsty. Contemporary sources to Shakespeare often refer to Cade as "Irish" because that was (and in some places still is) a shorthand for brutish, senseless violence. This makes me so sad, and for myself, Cade had become a way of thinking about our lost radical heritage.

Raptures & Captures

Raptures & Captures is the final book in an original trilogy of works, written in collaboration with collage artist Steev Burgess. It remains my favourite of the three, and across an erratically prolific career, one of the books I am most proud of. I think this is because it touches a raw and vulnerable place in me; because it engaged my own profound yearning for the radical reciprocity invoked by saintly intercession.

The book did not begin with this stated intention. It began merely with my desire to write something about the vivid and surprising lives of the saints. I have always been spellbound by Catholic iconography, by martyr pageantry, and by the medieval Passion Play. I wanted to write poems that engaged with and evoked the striking visual language of those things, and which incorporated the fantastical and grotesque elements of hagiography.

However, as the book developed, and I spent time in the company of the saints, I began to understand something of the promise they extend to us; about the invigorating and subversive potential of their stories. I began to see the saints as guides, as fallible fellow sufferers, as tireless spiritual actors working on our behalf; as radical examples of struggling humanity who might show us how to bear with pain, how—in the words of Saint Silouan—to keep our minds in Hell and despair not.

While **Raptures** figures the saints in playful and idiosyncratic ways and across a number of modern contexts, they aren't "subversions", or secular reimaginings. There are, as the late Sean Bonney noted: 'traditions of thought that are interested in serving power. And [...] traditions of thought that are interested in freeing people from that power. Sometimes these traditions overlap. And sometimes they can be useful in both directions.' Christian belief is one such tradition, the real insurrectionary power of which poetry has only infrequently acknowledged or tapped.

The final section of **Raptures**, 'Prayers and Maledictions', began with my reading of Psalm 88 (the only Lament Psalm not to resolve itself in praise), and its impetus was the hopelessness of Tory Britain in the year 2019. I find it incredibly difficult to read those poems now because I had far from succeeded in not despairing. And yet, I believe there's a power and a purpose in the inconsolable lament. It becomes a place of protest and profound ethical questioning; a form of witnessing and deep solidarity. There is no catharsis to those poems: no one is let off the hook; no one is hoodwinked into believing something seismic and tangible has taken place, or been magically resolved by an empathetic sigh. Is that not what prayers are for?

Saint Silouan's injunction has often reminded me of Gramsci's riff on Romain Rolland: 'pessimism of the intellect, optimism of the will.' Which is not merely a clear-eyed understanding of how bad things are, but an acknowledgement that the conditions for revolutionary change do not yet exist. Such change, for Gramsci, could only be brought about through organised, disciplined action. Gramsci's "hope" is a verb and not a noun. It exists only in its active expression. This is what I and others lose sight of at times: this sense of hope as something we do and not something we feel. Lament can remind us of this. That we should be seeking, not reasons to be hopeful, but ways of *being* hopeful.

A prayer is not an adult form of woolly-brained wishful thinking, not individualistic and passive, not an ongoing distraction from the work we are called to do. The saints show us this too, I think. They are, above all else, active agents of social change.

All three books are brought together here for the first time with some edits and additions, and without the original illustrations. In one sense, I am sad to lose them; they remain an important part of the poems' original creation and transmission. But it is time for these words to stand, unsupported. What you make of them now is entirely up to you.

/
Muses & Bruises

Poems by Fran Lock

I want freedom, the right to self-expression, everybody's right to beautiful, radiant things

—Emma Goldman

Contents

Muses & Bruises

An updated introduction..*i*

Melpomene..1

Euterpe, 1953..3

Thalia..5

Clio..7

Erato..10

Urania/Ourania..11

Polhymnia..14

Terpsichore..15

Calliope, 1985..16

+

On Modern Muses..17

Rag Town Girls

Rag Town..21

Rag Town Girls do Poetry..23

Rag Town Girls are Star Fuckers..25

Rag Town Girls go Dancing..26

Rag Town Girls do Unemployment..27

Rag Town Girls see God 28

Rag Town Girls Don't Want to be in your Shitty Fucking Magazine/
Anthology/ Stable of Wanky, Middle-class Poets Anyhow 29

+

On Rag Town Girls 31

Notes on the Muses 33

An updated introduction

By Fran Lock

Most people ignore poetry because most poetry ignores most people.

—Adrian Mitchell

I've got a lot of love for the late Adrian Mitchell, but I think he was wrong about this. I didn't have much access to poetry growing up, but that wasn't because poetry was *ignoring* me, that was because poetry had been deliberately engineered out of my life. I had never been told that poetry was *for* me, that I was allowed poetry, entitled to poetry, deserving of poetry. No one ever told me how much I *needed* it. And I did need it. We need it. All of us.

I came to poetry alone, late, and by chance. My first feeling at having found this *beautiful, radiant thing* was a mixture of exhilaration and relief, rapidly followed by a burning rage that something so essential, so sustaining; something so rich in sweetness and in meaning had been kept from me. I carry that rage with me still.

Accessibility (or lack of it) isn't a matter of individual aesthetic choice on the part of the artist; the closing of doors is systemic and structural, it turns on inequality of opportunity and provision. By which I mean, poetry does *not* ignore people, but there *is* a system at work designed to exclude people *from* poetry. People like me. People like you. It starts at school, with a hidden curriculum that attempts to circumscribe and manipulate the cultural expectations of working-class kids by telling them what is and isn't *for* them. It has everything to do with the managed decline of Arts and Humanities subjects across all levels of education. It is rooted in the marketisation of the academy towards the exclusion of poor and working-class people. It is deeply embedded in the way successive generations of Tory governments have used so-called educational "reforms" to routinise and shrink the teaching of English in general and poetry in particular in schools, producing a loveless conveyor-belt curriculum where students are rewarded for the relentless memorising of disconnected facts, and discouraged from developing any kind of lively or critical conversation with and about literature.

Instead of placing the responsibility for engagement on the shoulders of already over-burdened creatives, our conversations should revolve around the tremendous amount of damage done by Michael Gove as Education Secretary in 2013, and Ofqual's equally scarring 2020 decision to make poetry optional at GCSE level. This is an ongoing and ideologically driven process, symptomatic of the last Tory government's myopic and grimly utilitarian focus on STEM subjects within the academy, and their entirely political determination to concentrate the burden of that skewed focus on poor and working-class people.

In 2022, the Office for Students announced plans to remove funding for "low quality" courses, which they defined as those where less than 60% of participants go into "good" jobs or further study quickly after graduating. This has led to a number of universities—among them Sheffield Hallam, Cumbria, Roehampton, and UEA—suspending or cancelling Arts and Humanities courses amid budget cuts and spiralling redundancies. The idea seems to be to strongarm universities (with a particular emphasis on non-Russell Group universities) into vocational courses, thereby shrinking at one stroke the pool of contributing talent to the artistic and cultural life of this country to a small group of privileged graduates. This is the climate and the context for "most people's" disengagement with poetry.

You can't be a poet, people said to me. No, because heaven forefend I should aim so high, heaven forefend I should have such an unrealistic ambition as to acquire language, to articulate and to express myself. No, because if I—as a marginalised or oppressed person—acquire that language, develop that skill, then I am arming myself. If I am articulate then I cannot be discounted and I will not be ignored. If I have access to the written word, then I am connected to the whole world, I can build movements, I can move mountains, I can understand the nature of that which keeps me down. Language is a sword and a shield; if I am dexterous with language, then I understand how language is used to ensnare and enslave me; I know when I'm being lied *about* and when I'm being lied *to*. If I have poetry, I have a voice. If I can think for myself, speak for myself, then I can define myself and represent myself. That is a dangerous and wonderful thing.

Better for some if art and culture remain behind high fences in self-policing middle-class enclaves. They'll stuff my head with shit instead, tell me I'm fit for bread and circuses, disposable dross. Give us stunted words for ugly lives, because we're "rough", because we're "stupid". Because it's what we "want", all we have the capacity to enjoy.

We're not stupid. I love language. I love poetry, *all* poetry: the Lais of Marie de France, Chaucer, Milton, Blake, Clare, Keats, Yeats, Fiacc, Plath, Brookes, all of it. I reclaim it, I appropriate it, I snatch it back as an act of daily, defiant radicalism. It *all* belongs to *all* of us.

And language belongs to us, in all its complexity and richness, in all its rolling, roiling musicality. I was told once that my writing was "inauthentic" because working-class women don't think or speak that way. Bollocks. I *am* a working-class woman, and I *do* write and think and speak this way. There is no one homogeneous working-class voice, any more than there is a single monolithic working-class culture or identity. No one has any right to set proscriptive limits on the way we sound or the words we use.

In any case, poetry is artifice. It's not merely a sieve for lived experience. It's a site of experiment and play, not an unfiltered document of consciousness. We craft with as much deliberation and care as our middle-class peers. We have our own deep aesthetic basis.

The poems in this collection revel in richness and in strangeness, they positively wallow in it. I don't apologise for that. I won't strenuously enact anybody else's vision of working classness; I assert my right to be lavish, to be complicated, to be "difficult". The poems are about beauty and meaning, and the unlikely places working-class women and girls find these things, the unlikely materials from which they are composed. They sing with survivalist swagger. It's an excess of expression driven by a poverty of means. It's our decadence. It gives me life.

Emma Goldman is often misquoted as saying that without dancing it's not her revolution. I'd go further, without dancing (or poetry) there is no revolution of *any* description. We have to first recognise our right to joy, to pleasure, and ourselves as agents and creators of this joy. Poetry is always waiting—go and claim it.

Melpomene

And he says I have this hardly-original
hole inside of me; that I am two things
infinitely: carnal and futile. He's right.
I am a bad wife, a wanting quarry
of witless worry; lank rage, grim schlock,
and stroppy poverty. I am sleazed in
the green of The Land, raining down
her birdsong in blows. The dubby
crush of my keening does his head in.
I sink kisses into screams like pushing
pennies into mud. And he says he is *done*.
From the wordy murk of my loss come
lanterns and daggers, and I am my country:
mean, gutless and Mediaeval; a dread
mess of battlements and spoils. He cannot
love me, grieved to my gills and grinding
exile like an axe. He cannot love me,
howling out my mutant blues to no one.
My semi-automatic sobbing wakes
the neighbours. I am sorry. I have tried
to live lightly, to live like *gadje* girls,
to make my mouth an obedient crock
of homage; to keep my swift hands soft
in illiterate peachiness. But I am from
an ugly world, an ugly world with ugly
songs for busking in an underpass. I am
not one your machine-washable muses,
my face a cotton swab. I cannot come
clean, come cosy, come tame and fond.
His suckling fund of human love destroys
me. I am not good. I am a ferreting girl
who steals from shops, a perfidious febrile
girl who gobs off bridges; a hedging

and fretting girl, one eye on the exit.
I am *terrible*. I drink myself to a fly-
tipped farrago of falling down. No decorum
in me. My mourning is eloquent strumpetry,
and ruin porn will always be the whole
of my Law. I am sorry. And he says he
cannot love me in my insolent libidiny;
my shrill pandemic ditties: poems bleating
like woebegone ringtones. He cannot love me
in my words, raptures dragged from the slangy
waste of Norn. He says he will have none,
when a poem is a viral fire that spreads my anger
round; a typo-tastic war grave in which I bury
my dead. And he says I am *damaged*. I frisk
the heart for sadness, find it waiting
like a toothache. It is true. Thrice fool girl,
dangled at a day's end, what have I got
besides? There is only this particular fire
in me, this brief biotic craze of light, a halo
like a yellow enzyme: luciferase, fanatical,
and *dragging us down*, he says. He leaves
and slams the door. I breathe again. The T.V.
leaks a sour myrrh meaning evening. I scuff
my breath on the edges of an empty room.
Here is the moon, poor feme sole,
and the orange stars in their cold swoon.

Euterpe, 1953

I should tread *carefully*; these village women envy
me my revels, and when the Ten Bells has called time
their husbands come, to sway like charmed snakes
on the green. They come to drink poitín, to weave
and rail among the harebells and the broom. They come
to me, and I will not refuse them. I am all they have
of music.

And all men must have music, those young bucks bailing a song
from the depths of their bellies like water from a sinking boat;
even their fathers, starched in isinglass and prayer, who live
by discipline and thrift, for omens and for rosaries. They have
need of music too, for the swift physic of a poem; for shanties,
canting, bawdy psalms, all liming the throat like scalded milk.

I step into the centre of a circle in my silks, my skirts skirl
and madden, and the darkness dares a dance; the sky is crazy-
paved with stars. My hands are a hotbed of sovvies. I gather
my garlands and thalers, and twist, red and orange, inflammable
abandon. My flute blooms like a thorn-apple, pollenates an air
from woozy succour and rare night breath.

And we begin to surge and solve in rhythm. My music is
the flesh laid bare; the body is a song made flesh. The men
are getting creaturely, their voices peeled and keening out
in tune. This ransacked swim of heat and sweat is all we have
to prove we live. And I will corrugate praise in the teeth of dying.
Lament is a false friend. Revel is an engine, pumps the blood.

But I should tread *carefully*; these village women envy
me my revels, and when their husbands skulk to cold beds,
old scores and cold mutton, I'm alone, and I know well
how each kiss to its repercussion travels. In the early light

of morning those pious biddies throw their stones, the menfolk holding torches as my gleaning dance unravels. Ever thus, but when they come, then I will not refuse them. No, I will not refuse them, I am all they have of music.

Thalia

I couldn't decide whether to get a tattoo of a pegasus or a unicorn
and he says it's not *a* pegasus it's just Pegasus capital P definite article
and so I say well what is the name for a winged horse then?
and he didn't know and anyway in the end I went and plumped for
a wicked corolla of violet stars.

This other time his mouth a boozy gizmo pressing into mine and the boys
at the bus stop Jason especially langered long tongues out a country mile
and perving away without whit one of shame and so busy looking up my
skirt they didn't see Mad Ganley coming along the road his scrumpy face
skinned by the moonlight as it were an apple peeled to reveal its brown bits
and nasty bruises.

And I think it's better to be merry don't you? and I was snaking and laddering
and he was coming alive like a rope trick under my hands and I said I don't
love you love you or anything but please baby be my fifth business and he was
pressing on my moles like a rosary like he was keying in his pin and my body
was this big fleshy ATM or something and I opened my mouth and laughed
and I half expected a pageant of sodden fivers to fly out and hit him in the face.

Best of all though best of all though best of all is the girls my sisters
when we go out all shiny eyes and Dimonique drinking our

trinketyskinful
and our forte is floozy and rare auld times and in the fluorescing plenty
of the club when we're writhing as one like a Hindu deity so many pairs
of bangled wrists hennaed hands and *he* says kiddo I wish there was more
of me to go round and I sing never ever such devoted sisters and we're
gorged on the dance spliffy vixens going down in an April shower of hijinx
giggles and cheap Lambrini.

Clio

My mother was a Goddess, ash blonde
and sombre longing; she kept a wise tongue.

When memory was sewage
treatment work, the water lapped
over her elbows like opera gloves;
she wore green velvet and white
feathers—lushly augmented.

Her perfume was mock orange, zinnia,
syringa. Her nails were perfect; her breath
a wrangle of flowers.

My mother held on to our history—pinkly
strombus conch clutching the sound of the sea.

My mother was a Goddess, and when
she spoke a yellow light embellished
her head in a soft cartoon *Eureka!*

My mother whispered *home* and *road*
with the same exhausted tenderness of old
men blowing their warm
air into the nose of a spooked horse.

I am not my mother.
I must bawl and crow,
pulling the past from my head
like a hank of hair.

My wet brain is whoopee-squeezed
or wrung
out as a damp rag.

I fathom like a fishwife, live by *ruckus*
and by *flannel*; spring our stories
on strangers, clucking my shameless
payload patois—loony on the bus.

Poshrat, history is the sucked egg
my mouth won't hold. I have to speak
or else snap mad.

Oh, here are our ancestors, wide in all
their inundating deadness. They shriek
through me, or else I teem, ghostbusy,
a wicker creel, bulging.

I must speak of this, our dead,
swaying in an amnesty of bandages
and indefensible deeds.

They come by cudgel and succour,
by gutrot, gouging and secret melee.
I will speak of this. The dead will
have din, will have cadging and gadding
and endless clamour.

The dead will sing, a slurred flurry
of voices, slurry of voices. They are a chorus
for gallows and lynchings. A hanged man
is a string instrument; a caved-in infant
demands a thumped drum.

My mother was a Goddess, she could charm
bees and her cheekbones were stunning. Her silence
gathered dust like an heirloom.

I am an *unquiet child*. I see things
and I must tell:

that man, grinning out from under
the redacted oblong of his eyes, crawled
from the comic opera of the past, dragging
his period costume;

the shimmering child, a mirage,
his upturned face is filling with sleep
as a plastic basin fills with rain.

Erato

"I'm Miss World, somebody kill me"—Hole, 'Miss World'.

And to top it all off, I'm expected to ride on
a float, my face scraped on in a strong wind, all
tits and teeth, rigid as any hood ornament: winged
Victory, pigtailed and pinioned. Bow to the crowd
like Jackie O, glamming it up at an airport. Blow
them a kiss, sceptred Gretchen, bestowing my lip-
gloss right and left. Pah! Nothing's changed.
I could be one of those big-boned comely undulants
from back in Nana's day, a greyscale girl in stiff sateen,
rubbing the suds from her smile. Same naff spangles
anyway, same paste tiara, dollop face, congenial
and mooning. But oh, those were *healthy* girls, curly
and fey and easily pleased. Nana, with her Fanta-
shock of orange hair, pale as a plate of pressed curd;
a rosette pinned to her rubbery dugs by the mayor.
Yuck! The windy bag of his jowls an inch from her
upturned nose, and he gropes like a mole at her seed-
pearled bodice. Nana, a gattling girl, content to prate
world peace and happy marriage 'til the cows came
lowing home. But I am not *healthy*, not *happy*, not safe
in the jammy past. I am myself, and only myself:
specimen of soothsaid youth, the dispensable
and disarranged. My bones lack calcium. My life
lacks direction. I am only myself, prized from the ant-
farm farce of social housing, and held to the light
like a counterfeit coin. A brazen fake and everybody
knows it. Not *lovely* but *typical*. A karaoke beauty,
only fit for generic reels and green streamers. My compact
mirror shows a sad wan, cornered by exhaustion, too tired
to turn being stared at into an art form. Gawp at the camera.
Pink pout pops in a flashbulb like gum.

Urania / Ourania

i

Tonight there is a storm and Reverend Mother
has confiscated all our magazines!

Reverent Mother, in the half-light through her open
door, looks like a thin, green candle. She carries
a patterned birch and a psalter, God and his much-
gilded invective.

Because she took our magazines I will do the casting. I am
better than the magazines, their guesswork and dappy fashions.
When you turn over the cards you must keep your Fate Hand
steady. It is like playing Operation. No, it is like taking an eyelash
out of your own eye with needle-nosed tweezers.

Tonight there is a tempest, as in *The Tempest*, and I
am casting. First I must shut up my swarmy thoughts.
I disappear into the vanity cabinet – skin diver pursuing
a pearl, a pill, a plaintive string of pills, lined up in
a long chain, hoaxing a rosary.

Now I am ready. Tonight the island is wild.
A cormorant is a silk purse for a portion of storm.
I watch the cormorants fold away their wings, closing
up their bodies like gibbets. My head is hollow with vision.
My thoughts caught in the halogen strip like flies. I am
wearing my own hair as a hood. I am going to begin
my predictions:

Tonight there will be hurricanes! The Gods in a starry
lather, goaded into escapades. I am astrological, precocious
with omens. I name the girls their terrible husbands: eight

madding bastards who go to the drink and drive their fast
cars into quarries.

And the school, our Reverent Mother: five years' time
and the novices with their currying, sheepish looks will
all be gone, their frailties and their waltzes swept massively
away.

ii

The Little Sisters in their clerical caterwaul, hang
lullabies like lanterns in the rafters of the roof.

The girls here get a skin on like boiled milk.
They sponge or drudge, or sob into their stirabout,
chewing the ends of their hair.

I once tried to explain the heat death of the universe
by muddling jam into Emmeline's porridge. She hit me
with a wooden spoon.

Tonight it is raining. They were aiming paper darts
at the Pavee girl, her *pasty face* is a chalky streak,
like birdshit on a black-out curtain.

Maybe tomorrow they'll find her narrow body in the narrow
bath, stood out against the dark water like the white blaze
on the nose of a black mare.

Or maybe she'll ascend to the stars, open
the window, climb onto the ledge. Behind her the girls
all cold-creaming each other's faces, singing along
to a smuggled B-side, egging her on to *fly away
home.*

Those girls, embroidering biology with tissue and excuses,
mouthing moist idiocies at one another: *a pash, a crush, she
spat, she cursed me.* Giddy, winsome girls. And stupid.

She always liked the drastic math of distances, distances
measured in the number or holes you can fall into
at any one time.

I once tried to explain the heat death of the universe
by spooning jam into Emmeline's porridge. She hit
me. And she hit me. And she hit me.

Polhymnia

And I will bend to my service, dancing bear
in her hair shirt, slowly swayed. I am built
for scourges, fasts, and sacerdotal tasking;
for squirming thirst and high compline. I
offer up this song, my song, the big-haired
power ballad of my penance. Do not hide
your face away, oh Lord, but play the long
odds of my rescue; adjust your cloth cap,
pull on your nubby gloves, and work
the short—oh, shortest—con of my salvation.

I will stoop to my service, Lord, pretend to
a prudent recluse; to six degrees of picturesque
scrimping. Ashy-faced, crone, and erring, I
will submit. And I shall commit my lipstickless
singing; kneel with parabolised saddos, hooded
like hawks. Lord, do not turn away from me.
My narrow bed is a plank for walking, nightly.
And Sister Joan, that fat, canonical chatelaine,
crouches behind my keyhole, a fell vigilante,
full of condensed milk and malapropped spite.

Yes, I will sing in my service. When I sing
Paradise pulls from the true like a Polaroid
picture in candled resolve. This is the real
work of serving, not sweeping up our sighs
in a sooty house. Praise is rough contraband,
colours the lung; is yarning an *ave*, red thread
and gold.

Terpsichore

No, not those girls, in a pink-white crisis of coquetry, whose movement is all anatomical trance. Not those girls, in crêpe and tulle, and transports; trippy telepresent swan maidens, dizzied at a ritual, whose wings are a pillow fight frieze of feathers, who dither and spin. No, not them. I will have quarrelsome harbingers, stripped to their strict funery, caustic and wan, whose dance is a railing intercourse. I will have symmetry, a plague of symmetries. Our faces are beacon and I will shine, louche and bruised, enshrined in a tiered dress, in a webbed mass of antisocial black. Our faces are *vévé*, brute and greased. Our bodies will verge and rivet and churn. This is to be a haggling dance, a dance of harm and prayer. I will not dance with the frittering girls, pointing their snug toes, truffled in gentrified petticoats, their small paws pandered in lavender laps. Mine are the serpent cohort, twisting into heated coils, superbly Tesla. My chorus is *street meat, puta madre, valley trash*. We gloss a dance without music, the mouth an alchemical smear. The heavy night has a headache. We are a human heatwave, heat-weaved. Writhe to the cadence of a knife fight, dear.

Calliope, 1985

Here it is then, girls. I'm wise enough to know when to quit, are you? Sweet girls, bonny and frantic, damning yourself with incredulous hexing. The coppers will come, as bent as spoons. Regardless, the coppers will come. Pig bastards, fascist fucks, as pushy as stage mothers. This operational egging on is endless. This one, a diva, preening his fists like a song. He's out for you, sweet girls. Pack up your homes, pack yourselves into yourselves, your sleeping bags, your agonies and cabbages. Your van is a bin of cinders now, they've lit fires under us. This field is a charmed steppe, glows, is sodden and welling. Our cars, our vans, our homes are nodes of light. Oh sweet girls, go, through a gap in the fence, through the shoved rummage of bodies, the boys in the blame of their bodies, slumming in mud. Pass Danny, a mummy-wrapped Murphy in his sea-dog dreads, his mouth a crush, a smear, a frail scrape. Boys, girl, the dogs in their consort swarm, snapping their teeth, perforate urgently. The dogs profess a music, proliferate vexed howls, homesick. Those pig bastards, Nazi fucks, breaking heads. This one is virtuoso, trebles the black keys of our teeth like a Mozart. Girls, the radiant pain of a burning. A scheme of trees, black against yellow, and red, and run. I will stand my ground, stirring these fault-lines into my face, stirring tamarind and turmeric into my pot. I mother regret, lug love like a missal, am passive, impassive, and just. Here it is then, walloped, tackled and cracked, auditioning sleep. Leave me inlaid like a Gibson guitar, acoustic and mournful and mother of pearl.

On Modern Muses

These Muses are Traveller women, but I don't see these poems as being about "Travellerness" any more than they're poems about "femaleness" or the business of being a woman. There is, at any rate, an elasticity and capaciousness to both terms, neither identity is definitive, safe, or stable.

Who decides what it means to belong? Inside identities or bodies? The ascription of meaning is a function of power. If our names do not belong to us—if we are powerless—then how do we live with the labels of others, at the mercy of meanings we did not create, names we did not choose.

The identities of the nine Greek Muses have morphed and warped over time; tailored and shaped to serve the private peccadilloes of artists and the hidden agendas of culture. In this way they share a common history with all women, but especially with those women who represent the feared and fetishised "o/ Other".

These are poems, then, about o/Otherness; about how those who inhabit this o/Otherness work with and against the representations, taboos, and meanings they've been branded with. These are poems of resistance, poems in which the antagonists subvert, pervert, reject and celebrate these varied versions of o/Otherness to create and recreate themselves. This process is full of wit and play, but it also has its coercive variants. It can also be endlessly iterative, compulsive, exhausting.

To be o/Other is to be an object of both fantasy and scorn, to embody in equal measure the exotic and the fearful, private lust and public shame; the objectifying gaze and the annihilating stare. These poems explore that contradiction, that hypocrisy, and what it does to those who live with it and within it. These poems advocate for dancing and for singing, for the capacity of poetry to give us a language in which to define ourselves, a way of using a hegemonic language like English that does not feel like an obscure form of betrayal.

Ultimately, these poems are about the friction between exclusion and imperfect assimilation, about the gaps between self and society in which we make a life.

Rag Town Girls

Rag Town

Chorus: Us learned the truth at seventeen, that love was made for beauty queens, and silly cows who all believe the shit they read in magazines...

The man on the corner screaming: *Who'd you think you are?* And La-la was scared of him, so I kicked him square in his Sassenachers, and *fuck you very much* for my pains. No one is here for the fun of it. La-la and I going down the offie in pessimistic leggings with the knees bagged out because who cares anyway and why make the effort? This is the only *forever* we'll ever get our hands on. No *love*. There's no one here on whom to lavish absolutes. *Love*, the defeatist fan-fic of amateur porno; the dropped jaw you drag on gravel. La-la says *we was never not hungry.* Sometimes we just stay in and listen to music; we like the shy boys, furtively genderless, pouting their lisping aggro at no one. La-la lines my eye for me. My slow blink is target practice. La-la's lips are flytrap pink, then red, and green. We're rendering, extraordinary with war paint. In La-la's room, sub-tropically postered, glossy leaves that wilt in scented heat. We've closed the windows. *Halleluiah* happens. Slow dance in odd socks. We move, distorted buoyancy. La-la's is a calm she wears like a scar. In the flat above they're screaming, a rage that sounds like running water. Constant torrent, force of nature. We smoke, we're getting slow. La-la picks her words like eyelashes. I pursue my words with tweezers. *Never connect*. We're staying in, not for us the strident delinquency of pulsing beats and pity fucks. Ned, his catastrophic handspan through a window in a pub. C and K and all the rest, buzzing like a game of Operation. The guilty hurt you grasp like a rose between your teeth, else slips between your ribs in an opportune alley with a boy's hand on your thigh. La-la is beautiful. By which I mean La-la is La-la, and when we lie side by side we look like we belong together—two halves of a worm that got sliced by a spade. A prayer might go like this: *Let summer not become the migraine that divides us.* Gross old men peering from behind expectant hedges. Dads that hassle us in shorts. But La-la most because I am gargoyle. A prayer might be something to do with escape. But that's not realistic. We can only run so far. The elasticity of anger, madness pushed to a tinfoil extremity, howling at the moon outside the city limits. But just outside. There is no road to trip. There is no bird's eye view. La-la is asleep. Sister from another mirror, how I've wanted in every sense repulsed enthralled the pinkish meat of you. La-la, when my jaundiced labours end and I return, empty-handed, artlessly sullen, will you always be waiting? No. There is no *always*. Rag Town's raving its face off again. The neckline plunges darkly. The pencil pushes back at the hand that holds it.

Rag Town Girls do Poetry

The boys was predictably lingering. You, flea-market demeanour, not benign, not even really joking. Your dress is guesswork: *sheer* is the word. I have the scarecrow's hurt mufti, a grudging velvet, wet black soil, and I have the eye's glassy art, will *screw 'em out*, the other girls, with beauties we will never have recourse to. The boys was banging on, tactless and awed, all smirking grievance, saluting the stiff red pout of you. You said: *I dunnae aim t' please*. They looked at you and trembled. Boys, girls, flaunting a mere shruggable illness. We was the two-headed Goddess of Anything Chronic. We was *a couple a' canny twats*. You trampled roses under foot. I bit the heads off bats. The hardman had a blue tattoo, a pulpy laugh. You planted your slippery, ill-advised mouth right on his thick, hot jugular. These were dark times, a bad idea was *really brilliant*. Your breath an ashy blessing as you said: *fuck me incurable in a nylon light*, with a sigh like artificial sweetener. My eyes was mood rings, mood swings, changeable and squeamish, pulsing waves of earnest malice, the shit I was eager and toxic with: Indigo! Indigo! Indigo! You took my hand in the ladies, you used a nail to trace my vein. I got a crawly lust inside of me. I got the urge to open up, to decorate with blood's black bunting, all across the mirror. You wrote: *Gimme a fix!* On the glass with a lipstick, in a richer colour than the one I run with. Omegaless, my vegan saline, super-unleaded, a diet shake. You was laughing, and I locked on you: gaunt, ecstatic, bandying about like a dying swan. You, haughtiness, promiscuous swank; a grin like a lizard: from rust to gold, cold-blooded rhetoric, sea-change, disco. You was an unpronounceable name, more night than shade, and I was lusciously poisoned. The boys was boohooing into their cups. You was the near-death dazzle of cheekbones. I was in the spotlight like an ant under a magnifying glass, tiny black body about to fry. You was as cool as a crock sink, you was wearing running water in the shape of male tears. You was paragon and ghastly like a figure on a tomb. I was a gargoyle, yellow and crumbling, croaking with a gap-toothed, boggle-eyed discord. We was cackling like witches; I was hooked and stooped and skinny; you was all shook up with mega-mega sorcery. When we was up at the front a straggly clarity came inching across my brain like a sprig of barbed wire. All eyes was sucked towards you, all their metal fillings was drawn in glittering file towards your powerful magnets. You was lit up like a super villain. I was your hunchbacked assistant. You made the lightning crack, and I mopped up the electrical spills. When we was done you gathered my arms like firewood, and the boys goggled, and the girls goggled. You super-collided my forehead in a kiss. La-la, who loves ya, baby?

Rag Town Girls are Star Fuckers

Because God, back then they was *so cool*. Everyone was *so cool*. And the frontman rolled up his sleeves in the spotlight, curling his lip back, flexing his risk. And we was *so cool*. And we wasn't screaming, we was sucking our cool enthusiasm up through straws. Mine's the murkiest rum in recorded history. La-la's on vodka, a tight, hot buzz you wriggle into. Because God, back then they was *so cool*. And he's talking to us. And we're talking to him. And my voice falls out of me, decanted in splashes. And when the men in torn black jeans carry the wide black boxes solemnly about it is like a funeral in a silent film. He presides at a private grief, head turned away: half vampire, and half priest. La-la kisses his ring finger. The players of instruments assemble themselves like Argonauts, awaiting their turn. Because God, back then they was *so cool*. And our eyes was wide on a gluttony of dust. We lacked and murmured, wanted things. We was *so cool*. Undress, and the long spine jukes like a hare, yellow in a narrow sunrise in a hotel bedroom. *Cool*, worshipful and wooing. Bitten, kissed on, mawkishly convulsed; paused, posed in a roseate Polaroid. La-la is a white head on a black background like a pirate flag. And his songs like rancorous parables. And his hands in my hair. And his lip ring, septic metal; blissy swagger, we are punctured and crooned to. Oh, *so cool*. Girls with the plush breasts of pheasants, Flemish and still-life, artfully deceased. We pass between hands; we have the smooth green curvature of bottles. He pushes his thumb through me like an egg. The other boys make assaults on the satin.

Rag Town Girls go dancing

For the longest time, the face you palm like a precious stone, repeating the words *rose quartz* to yourself in an undertone. There was a love we ripened like amnesia, a big forgetting that filled in all the blanks. But then it was the afterward, the after wood: afflicted, skint, surplus and deserted in a world with too many women in already. On those days what else to do but squat before your bijou vanity table and make unflinching inventory, from mishap to disaster. On those days you apply green goo in a semi-circular motion, leave for fifteen minutes, then peel your face away from your face like the skin from hot, boiled milk. On those days you get ready. On those days you go out. *Out* isn't what it used to be: here comes C and C's disaffected pronouns, lungs crushed up like empties inside C's binder. C swaggers with the bullish musk C's drunk on. C swaggers. K swaggers. Everybody swaggers. *Out* is our brash disorder. *Out* is the gory logic we've feathered our brains with, everybody waiting for a violent shock. K holds out her hand for one split atom, two, three, an anti-social sufficiency of pills. Lukewarm worming dusk, and the club is getting moody, zoological. That happens. In the dark the faces of your girlfriends glow like orange pips: white, Americanly ominous, terminally undelighted. *Out* is grabbing La-la's hand and running through the green emergency exit to score a more decaffeinated atmosphere; it's laying your head in her lap in desolate homage, sucking the red wine stains from her sateen skirt. *Out* is the few loony stars on your walk back home, fading all patchy like a temporary tattoo. *Out* is the brittle, twitching fanfare blared from phones across the fountain, not quite 'Careless Whisper' as you kick off your shoes and declare undying lust. *Out* is you, belligerently messianic in the mid-nineties, La-la howling *come down* as you climb the Spire to death or glory. *Out* is more or less fucked; it's a fight with baldies, sleepy-eyed as stoics on the nightbus, in the lanes. It's you, Titan with head-wound 'cause you was spewing the sulphurous morning up, 'cause you wanted the world, 'cause you couldn't keep your big mouth shut.

Rag Town Girls do Unemployment

Somnambulous afternoon, slump-buttocked and grouchy. C'mon Ned, and you and La-la drag him off the couch. The high-street is sniffable, gluey, leaves your appetite in shreds, but anyway. And you're passing the burger bar, and the residents are foddering like zombies inside, and through the plate-glass you can see a woman, mid-forties, has cancer, her head all swollen, white and gummy like a sucked dumpling. And Ned remembers his Ma and wipes his nose on his sleeve. It's afternoon alright, with emergency services making a rock opera out of helicopters; a front bumper on a traffic island, gleaming like a horse's jawbone, picked cold. Incident tape extends anemone tendrils with a deep-sea delicacy, yellow, black and blue. Cars up on bricks are basking like sharks. The pawn shop with its windows smashed, a mayday of semi-precious metals, Community Support looking on like daffodils in high-vis. This is the world. You follow the one way system out of town. You're *going where the weather suits your clothes*, this from La-la, laughing. In the park you loll on the smogged up grass, or slouch on incoherent benches, grimed with arbitrary passions, and with birdshit. You share a tepid tea, watch junkies disappearing down into the public toilets like white rabbits, consulting invisible watches, muttering under their smeggy breath how *late* they are. It's as afternoon as it's going to get, the park becomes capered with dogs off leads, an English bull with his log-flume face makes a fuss of you. He is white all over, with a Gorbachev birthmark in brilliant raspberry. You decide to adore him. The women come next, stylishly adrift but miserable with it, their hair ornate in failure, scrape-backed and flammable, they dangle kids like shoulder bags, customised toddlers with teeth as straight as the edge of a credit card. They whoop but do not smile, a mannered joy they act out like an injury. You decide to go home, take a shower, rinse the dreggy sweat you are disgusted by. In the shower the removal of hair is like the unblocking of a sink. Over your shoulder, La-la, intent on the mirror, undoing her make-up in chess moves; unwrapping her reflection like a crappy Christmas present.

Rag Town Girls see God

There he is, eyes half closed, doing the math of a difficult miracle, wrist-wearied, leaning into his swig, his pull of smoke. We assume he is God. He reminds us of a man we once knew: slender and insulted by life, mixing his blessings like strong drink, suicidally agile, tying a nimble noose the minute your back was turned. Not all kinds of pain are soluble in water, this is a thing God would know. There he is, polishing a bad mood like a monocle, in dive bars, erring on the side of squalor, as is usual, succumbing to a bleak urge now and then, a typical thrill, blood's red adventure, cuts himself or dallies a sulky vein. He's writing on a napkin. He's writing in the back of an exercise book on green graph paper. This gives his words a barometric feel. Poems, possibly. A long phrase escalates like science: pressure, rise and fall. There he is. We assume he's God. Who else could he be? His blue eyes like stains under black light, a half-smile through a vaporous reverie. He reminds us of a man who was always leaving his door ajar like *youthful promise unfulfilled*. He reminds us of a man, decisively hysterical in hospitals on Friday nights. We came to see him. La-la held his hand in an ambulance once, and other girls, entangled attentions he grew tired of and soon. We remember him, passed out at a party, Lugosian in repose, those folded hands, those overweening teeth. C had saddled him. Others too, young and drunk, with slack or sculpted mouths, trashy and vamping, pretending to be grown. God, yes. He absorbed their adoration like the sea absorbing snow. There he is, tremulous willpower, Crombie coat. When he wrote it down, when he pulled you to him in a bouncer's embrace. Love as a grunting headlock you cannot wriggle out of. Better to lie still, snug and grim against the reeling two-step of his heart. If he had a heart. La-la says yes. I am inclined to contrary opinion. Watch him now, groping at dominoes, putting forth paranoia like pine needles. He is the same, but elongated. There is prayer, and then there is a deadlier efficacy. God, in his Kingdom. God, in his Wisdom. God, in his window seat. He let himself go.

Rag Town Girls don't want to be in your Shitty Fucking Magazine/ Anthology/ Stable of Wanky, Middle-Class Poets anyhow

Writing a poem is not like painting a nail. But you like things with *proper edges*, words obscenely organised. We take our rejection letters to bed, spend weekends floundering a vowel, and *how to get this better?* Ours, the unstruttable slang of profitless margins. We belong on the out of things, prowling and gaspy. And picking a side is like picking a scab—the inner arm, its crumbs of blood—. Writing a poem no one wants. Insomnia's aberrant artifice, night after night. It is taking out an ad in the paper: *I have built my house of straw!* Our poems are prefab and flammable, no one's moving in. You like things with *proper edges*. The world is not something to traverse, but something to survive. To keep us on our toes the city varies its monsters, but sex keeps harping its long, fatal theme. *Residents*, but not *citizens*. *Relatives*, but not *family*. Blame is the only thing that belongs between us equally. La-la says the poem comes away from her like an enchanted shadow detaching. I disagree. I think it is more like tearing a plaster off a deep cut to the thumb. You like things with *proper edges*. You would never mistake *violation* for *volition*. In the bathroom mirror we try out our Poetry Voices. Poetry Voices are needed for the receiving of prizes. I've been perfecting a cough that sounds like crutches being kicked. La-la's laugh has stripped a turkey carcass down to the fats in under sixteen minutes. Now we need the outfits. We will wear white, immaculate as rabbits. La-la's is the Roman toga of the downward thumb. Mine is a sheet with holes cut in for eyes. Writing a poem is not like planting a kiss. Or a tree. How to get this better? Intelligence a sauce we suck from fingers, with fuck me haircuts in a youth club. How to slide right out of yourself, like a limousine pulling away from the curb? How to deny the flight of stairs you took to the roof on windy days, when you wanted to float, kite caught in a whiplash of its own making? How to fake it? How to keep it in, that jittery, impassable grief? *Don't scratch yourselves, girls. Bathe. Point your toes.* Glowing in a backward light cast by everything you flee from. You like *proper edges*, incline a tin ear to the shrug and flutter of our debateable music. If we could only sing like you, a proficient, accredited language. But we can't, so we won't. La-la lit a fire instead. It ate a hole in everything.

On Rag Town Girls, or: Rag Town Girls Still Don't Want to be in Your Shitty Fucking Magazine

We have the right, and we deserve the space in which to be angry. I started writing the Rag Town sequence with this one thought looping endlessly in my head. It's there still: neo-liberalism's blanket refusal of women's rage is an earworm that just won't quit.

The poems came about in the wake of International (Working) Women's Day, and my disillusionment with what I perceived, and *still* perceive, as an ongoing cultural project to make feminism palatable and popular, and in doing so leave behind those women and girls who are most in need of its revolutionary message. Still true. But worse is the absorbing, co-opting and rebranding of women's anger. We now live within a cake-and-eat-it-scenario where our rage is abject and rejected, or else recuperated as marketable fetish, as vaguely amusing folly, as T-shirt slogans and sassy catchphrases, as two-dimensional "bad assery". Somewhere along the way it became unacceptable to openly acknowledge how class dynamics contribute to sex-based oppression, to say that women are a class cohort, exploited as sources of domestic, sexual, and reproductive labour; stymied by a visual culture created by and for men.

While mainstream feminist movements urge greater participation inside of the capitalist money-system as an avenue to freedom and self-fulfilment, we desperately need a feminism willing to identify capitalism itself as the fulcrum of women's exploitation. We need a perpetual labour shutdown, not accommodation within a life-denying system that fucking hates us.

I've brought this up often down the years and with each repetition it has been seen as more and more divisive. It's "divisive" to demand a version of feminism that isn't about individual choice and personal "empowerment" but collective liberation, for *all* women, not just rich pretty white and able-bodied ones.

This *still* fills me with despair. I wrote Rag Town to articulate that despair, but also to celebrate working-class girls, their artistry and voice, their unpredictable and vibrant networks; how we enrich and sustain each other and ourselves.

Rag Town became a place in which the joys, frustrations, miseries and victories of imperfect, unacceptable and angry women could be told. The poems speak of grind, grot and exploitation, but from the inside, with swagger, tenderness and élan. There's a refusal to give in, a determination to spin through their difficult lives and less than lovely town. This spirited resilience is something I've aspired to in my own life, something I witness every day in my family and friends. The poems are meant to stand as testament to those people, to reflect the ambiguities, the hardships, and the pleasures of growing up a poor girl. The poems make a space for and honour our anger, but also our kinship, solidarity, and music.

The girls in Rag Town insist upon their right to be seen in other ways than as objects or as victims. In ways that are as complex, nuanced and profound as their middle-class counterparts. We don't get a lot of that inside of contemporary culture.

Fran, 2024

Notes on the Muses

'**Melpomene**' (the Muse of Tragedy): her "tragedy" is both the past she carries, and her violent separation from it. She is someone who cannot reconcile herself to the world or to her life as it is. The speaker is someone who cannot return "home" but who cannot make peace with the inadequacies of her present place either. Edward Said described exile as "the unhealable rift forced between a human being and a native place, between the self and its true home: its essential sadness can never be surmounted." I think Melpomene is caught between opposing poles of exile and assimilation, finding no native place, no site of solidarity.

'**Euterpe**', known as the "giver of delight" (Muse of Music, and later Lyric Poetry): one of only two specifically historical pieces. This poem came to me in response to a story I was told about the unsolved murder of two Traveller women, somewhere near Kilsheelan during the 1950s. I couldn't verify the story, and suspect it's something of an apocryphal tale, but its existence struck me as a kind of informal acknowledgement of the tensions and toxicities that bubble and boil beneath the surface of communal life. This is a poem about hypocrisy, bigotry and blame, but more importantly to me, it's a poem about how something that has great beauty, sweetness and meaning to the initiated can be degraded and debased by deliberate misinterpretation. It's a poem about drawing strength and pleasure from a frisson of risk, about the courage not to be cowed, about daring to dance. It's a poem about everything irrevocably lost in translation.

'**Thalia**' (Muse of Comedy): this is my favourite of the nine pieces. Her monologue is funny, but she knows it's funny, and we're laughing *with* and not *at* her. She has this hectic, slightly mad vivacity, which is an expression of her as yet undefeated desire to see and know and experience *every*thing. I love her for her headstrongness, her determination to spread joy and hijinks. For me, she also represents sorority, laughter being that which binds her sisterhood together. She uses a lot of theatrical slang because her personal style is pure Vaudeville. She is a composite of many of the teenage girls in my life. In their inventiveness, flare/flair and frivolity I find hope.

'**Clio**' (Muse of History): this is perhaps the most complex of the sequence. I was thinking a lot about the tensions and collisions between cultural heritage and personal past. In Ireland in particular, History is often glorious, while the private lives and living memories of people and of families are littered with miseries, disillusionments and griefs. Clio is constantly measuring herself and her own foreshortened perception of History against the grand ancestral memory her mother was the keeper of. She blames herself, uses the word *poshrat* (meaning "half-breed") imagining that if she belonged more completely to her culture and its traditions she would be able to access a better story, a better memory. The piece reflects my own ambiguous attitude to and fraught relationship with the myth of Ireland and Irishness. Also, implicit in the poem are questions about what constitutes a history at all, who gets to be enshrined in story; who and what is worthy of remembrance?

'**Erato**' (Muse of Erotic Poetry, Love Poetry, and of Mime): I imagined Erato as one of a long line of Miss Connemara contestants; a beauty queen never allowed to be anything but beautiful, expected to turn being looked at into an art form and not particularly pleased about it. She's the parallel of Thalia, but Erato is imprisoned by her identity rather than inspired by it. The beauty contest is, to me, one the most anachronistic and baffling aspects of Irish culture. It baffles the poem's speaker too, who feels herself enslaved to and engulfed by decades of stifling tradition. Erato is female sexuality exploited in the service of cultural myth. "Not *lovely*", she says, "but *typical*", although beneath the surface she is anything but. The idea of Mime in this context signifies to me a going through the motions, the making of a series of content-less and hollow gestures towards tradition. Erato knows she's not the image in the flashbulb, but equally she does not know what she might be without it.

'**Urania/ Ourania**' (sometimes the Muse of Astronomy, sometimes the Muse of Astrology, sometimes both): I cheated here, imagining the dual aspects of Urania/ Ourania as identical twins, two girls enrolled in convent school, one of whom is very much concerned with the illicit practice of casting the tarot, and her sister who is held in fascinated thrall by science. They embody the tensions between the "rational" and the magical or mythic world, but also between culture and occulture, personifying several kinds of "forbidden" knowledge (the tarot itself and the reading of signs and portents, the secret world of schoolgirls with its ciphers and private signs, and physics, the enormity of which is another kind of challenge to the dominance of religion). For me these two represent the ways in which knowledge survives and takes root, makes its incursions into a culture that is trying to stifle it or stamp it out. Urania sees "civilisation" itself as an unessential relic that will be "swept away". Her knowledge is older, but it will endure.

'**Polhymnia**' (Muse of Hymns or Sacred Songs): this piece occupies a similarly uneasy intersection between Catholic faith and Pagan tradition. She too has a secret inner life, but hers does not exist in subversive undercurrent, rather it is repressed, except at vital moments when she is allowed to sing; in singing the two halves of her heritage are allowed to synchronise, to co-exist. In singing she becomes whole. For Polhymnia, as for myself, all songs and acts of singing are inherently sacred and healing.

'**Terpsichore**' (Muse of Dance): my Terpsichore embodies everything that is menacing or destabilising about "o/Otherness". In her dancing there is a violence and sexual threat, a grim revelling in the role of dangerous outsider, of being beyond society, its expectations and constraints. That is not to say she is a "powerful" figure in the usual sense, but that, being denied legitimate power she nevertheless finds ways of exerting influence, of using peoples' assumptions against them. She is underestimated, so she cultivates that underestimation and turns it to her advantage. I am not interested in excusing the sexual exploitation of women with some catch-all notion of "agency", but I do want to write about the ways in which women and girls maintain their dignity, and the strategies they adopt that allow them to survive. Terpsichore's dancing is a strategy, it walks the knife-edge between violence and sexual desire, and in doing so gives vent to her rage.

'**Calliope**' (Muse of Epic Poetry and of Eloquence): of course Calliope has the last word. Hers is the only other poem with a fixed date. The action of the piece takes place at an eviction in 1985, recalling the now infamous Battle of the Beanfield, but the "battle" could be anywhere, and it echoes all such scenes, now too numerous to mention. There is something tongue-in-cheek about this piece. A Muse of Eloquence being given to multi-clausal swear streams is intended as humour, but also there's something about the brutality of the eviction that makes her overstep her role, that causes her carefully constructed persona to topple and break. There are some situations in the face of which language is inadequate. State violence is one of them. Calliope's battle closes the collection, but it also begins it again, in Tragedy, with Melpomene, and the things that she's seen that will not give her peace. In a way I wish I was ending on a happier note. I would have liked to give Thalia the last page, or Urania, or maybe even Terpsichore, but sudden and shocking displacement underscores every aspect of these women's lives. Not just Traveller women. Not just migrant women and refugees. All working-class women. Whose locatedness is never stable, always fraught. Calliope's piece is a reminder and a call to arms. Keep moving girls, keep searching, for a better belonging, a better road, a better home.

//
Ruses & Fuses
Poems by Fran Lock

"Omnia sunt communia" (everything belongs to everyone)

—Thomas Müntzer

Contents

Ruses & Fuses

An updated introduction..*i*

witchfinder's cabaret..45

you ask us why we fight..46

noisy john...49

turning earth..51

maschinenstürmer...52

public lecture..54

cade's chroniques...56

"and myscheff is nothyng redress"..57

a prophesy...59

lady chapel..60

æthelthryth..61

our (mother's) day will come...62

cable street 1936/1981..64

news from nowhere...66

great escapists #1..67

great escapists #2..68

on fighting on...69

fleet..71

+

the travesties...75

Notes on the poems..85

An updated introduction

By Fran Lock

I've been thinking a lot about history lately, so it feels appropriate to return to this collection now. Chiefly, I've been questioning what history is, and who has it? The rich have a history, certainly: their posterity is long. But such posterity is a form of posthumous luxury, thus seldom afforded to the poor.

There's something Arlette Farge says, about history being a 'collision of competing logics', that is still applicable here. By which I meant—I mean—that these poems are not, in any literal or linear sense, the story of English radicalism. I didn't want to write that book for two main reasons: firstly, because a coherent and cohesive "story" of English radicalism does not exist, and secondly because to spin as a straightforward line of descent something we can only ever experience as distorted, entangled, and fragmentary, is to elide the many acts of systemic intellectual violence done to our radical histories; is to ignore the many ways in which our access to the past is impeded, its faceted truth dulled, diluted or obscured.

Shortly after *Muses & Bruises* was released and the idea for this collection was being kicked around, I was asked by a friend why I wasn't writing a sequence based on the Irish radical traditions that inform so much of my own political thinking and occupy such large tracts of my emotional and imaginative space. In order to answer that question, I needed to go back to childhood, and to an English state school system where history came to us potted and piecemeal, portioned out into discreet periods named for their reigning autocrats; autocrats, it seemed, of largely irrelevant and undifferentiated character.

In state school history the role of the poor was to suffer, a motiveless mass at the mercy of larger happenings: privations, plagues, famines, fires, religious persecutions and insane moral panics. The effect was disjointed to say the least and could only ever afford us the merest fleeting glimpse of the lively dissenting communities that have underpinned and undercut English society on every level and at every historical turn. This is not so in Ireland. Ireland has its own fraught and freighted relationship to cultural memory and the historical past, but institutional—and institutionalised—amnesia about working-class dissent is not one of its problems. History, in Ireland, may be experienced as a nightmare, a prison, an acute psychic pain, but it is a history, nonetheless, in which people—the people—are prominent movers and shapers of their own divided destiny.

Working-class identity and history

This collection is more an act of imaginative archaeology, an exploration of and excavation into the lore and the legends of diverse radical histories. I am using the plural deliberately. There is no monolithic entity we can easily identify as Radical History. Movements diverge and intersect, interests collide and coalesce, logics compete for supremacy, contesting the cultural space. The poems in this collection are correspondingly crazed, bewildered and bewildering at times; composed from the sherds and shrapnel of a past, or pasts, both buried and scattered. I don't want to tell you about John Lilburne or Gerard Winstanley, I want to show you how I had to uncover them, warts and all, from the slimy sediment of state education in which they'd been immured.

This is a book about the ways in which we, as radicals, as working-class people, access our collective troubled histories, and the echoes and incursions those histories make into the present. This collection is about my own tentative, pre-internet inroads into those histories, uncovering my ancestors and unlikely allies, sometimes with beetle-browed bookish diligence, but more frequently through moments of serendipity: a song lyric here, a snippet of footage there, an adult conversation overheard, a urine-tinted clipping from a local paper, lining the rat cage, curling at both ends.

Working-class identity can be like this, I think. Our historical sense of ourselves, our movements, communities, voices, and myths are hedged with ambivalence, ignorance, and uncertainty. We have not, traditionally, been the authors or the archivists of our own experiences, our own stories. Not because we have nothing meaningful to contribute, but the exercise of history (as a subject and a discipline) requires literate leisure, a space for reflection not typically afforded to working-class people. Our stories have been kept from us, erased and eroded, but surviving in unlikely ways, in slang and songs, in long, unconscious cultural memory, spread on breath, by sound.

This fragmentation of our pasts, and our inability to apprehend our histories whole is deliberate, systematic and strategic. It suits elites that we see ourselves as on the outside; at the mercy of historical and economic forces we can neither resist nor control nor fully understand. This is a gilt-edged crock of shit. We are *not* rootless, nor powerless, nor alone. Working-class people have acted with agency, autonomy, creativity and resilience. We have suffered, but we have also survived, and each act of survival is a blueprint and a banner for the next act, and the next. The more we work to understand our own legacies and legends, the stronger our armour against the grand narratives those in power would feed us *gravage*.

We live in violent times. In times when the dead body of a working-class solider sent to die in an illegal war is worth more than a living working-class citizen engaged in unlovable labour, or worse still, unemployed. They have weaponised nostalgia, hijacked our past and tied it to deadly nationalistic scripts. I hate that. This collection means to honour memory, the act of remembering, and to interrogate with honesty the often unpretty processes by which histories are uncovered as we develop, collectively and individually, like a Polaroid photo, a sense of ourselves.

Fran, 2024

witchfinder's cabaret

come with me, and you will see such marvels. i will show you
the world turned upside down, a man steamed open like an
intercepted letter; fatalists raving with tapeworm, pining away
under house arrest. i swear, you will barely believe your eyes.
behold, cromwell's smirky ghost, embossed upon an obol! roman
general, warts and all. hail the conquering hero. here is a bone
for your buttonhole, a finger, fine and white. the perfect fit.
a grimoire bound in human skin. vaudeville and guignol.
a pyromaniacal chorus lines of spanish cardinals, swirling
their crimson capes like supermen, inebriated matadors,
psychopathic mountebanks. here is pestilence and heresy,
christ's glass eye, spinel-blue; a pewter crucifix. totems dug
from slug-befuddled borders in a kitchen garden. here is
a girl you can burn like a thin brown candle, bones for soup
and fat for soap. you will see such marvels. listen, a head
sings in its gibbet, like a linnet in a gilded cage. müntzer's
tongue is torn out at the root. müntzer, a protestant orpheus
singing. here, are the tournaments and corpses, *desperate
remedies*, swine grown fat on a basket of pearls. come with
me, you'll see the choicest ghosts: exiled princes, jaundiced
and paupering; young men drugged by hunger 'til they sway
like dancing bears. all will be revealed: novices crouched
in convent corners, sucking the soil from daffodil bulbs;
priests planted in shallow holes like blighted belladonna.
there's a body in the wych elm; inquisition, *kesseltreiben*.
there are men, stunted and covetous, teeming with fleas,
shaking their fists at the firmament. there are women
measuring bolts of cloth against the length of a human
scream. the bible is our centrepiece, lies on the table
like a slab of black bread. come see! come count these
grievous trinkets one by one: gold eyeteeth pulled up
with pliers, vulgate gouged in prison brick. the silver stud
still attached at his lip, curled at one end like a thin black fuse.

you ask us why we fight

i.m. Fergus O' Connor

you can make an inkblot of your nosebleed if you want to. talk and
tsk and suck
your teeth. conspiracy and crucible, and last of all is cliché: *fighting
irish*. tell me
how my fist offends propriety, then name me one good thing on earth
was ever
given freely. i'm a joke to you, but i have known a place where
mothers make
a theme song of their grieving. i've seen men kneel, not pious but
defeated; seen
them keen, with doffed caps, and tied tongues, and tugged forelocks,
far too long.
girls in gingham tabards, thin fingers rag-picked to an angry spasm;
our young
bucks buckled like broken ploughs after hard graft and heavy lifting.
you don't
want to know. so i swing, at gin-sickness, pittance and piecework;
flick-knives
and switchblades, imperfect contrition. i swing at the pitchy stink of
the barges,
at the pinch-penny portions of leprous bread; at itchy armpits, scarlet
fevers, at
scavenging, navvying, flimsies and chits. because this is *your* world:
bald men
dragging their knuckles across the middle distance. men with
tattooed dewlaps,
goosebumped in bermuda shorts, flying their stomachs and half-mast,
screaming
a *sieg heil!* into my face. there is nothing to eat, offal and porridge
and free
school meals. there's nothing to do, so brothers go obnoxious,

unwashed,
prodigal. or get themselves dead behind heritage. bygone pogrom, bad-debt,
self-doubt and ethnic cleansing. they took it to heart when you said you was better
than them. you took it too far when you said they belong to this doldrum squalor
and tenement dread, amphetamine pestilence, out of their heads, forever amen.
so i swing, i swing at the diesel and grease of an air we dare not breathe.
i swing at the mean-featured foremen, cussing and cursing and nursing their
two-ton grudges; at all of the *self-made men*, who expect us to *pull ourselves up*
by our punchlines, a racist slur with cowshit on our boots. i swing because
i'm sick of paedo priests and hanging judges; acid casualties, psycho-killers,
crouching like gargoyles in unlit stairwells, all straight razors and skinny
wrists. no one believes we are better than this. aspirant suicides, ceasefire
babies. brave new world, pimping its pockmarked acres of flesh in the shit-
witted gridlock of closing time, where *patriots* haggle for snatch in an alley,
and mullet-cutted absolutists traffic in retaliation, tracksuits and black-market
meat. deadbeat dads, slack-jawed and confecting endless fear against the sloping dark. oh, brave new world, of custodial no-hopers flogging stolen
stereos in multi-storey car parks. jerusalem. i swing, for little girls slurring
their homework. you called them *sluts*, you said they weren't worth

the sweat off satan's back, and now they believe. and now, those scallies
sharpen their hand- me-down swagger to a cutting edge. they'll cash your
cheque then spit in your shadow, leave you for dead. and you act surprised,
ask yourself why, while colicky longing fills the pigeon-chests of children.
while widows with twisted faces amplify bereavement with burlesque. a black
dress contriving a tactical malady. i swing, for the gaunt blunt-force of a pain
that breaks your back, for our remedial belief, the queasy bloated grief we march
in step with through the rankled light, the racing rain. born by summer's histamine
psychosis; bearing our fierce, inflexible shame. i swing, with my seldom succoured
brothers, sucker-punched, and always stuck somewhere between our conscience
and our cunning. Jerusalem. of dirges and of lurgies, sluggish nightmare, fumbling
drugework, men like you. justice, is a thin soup supped with a long spoon. small
wonder we fight, it's all we can do.

noisy john

i.m. John Lilburne

egotist. incriminated, pilloried, flogged with a three-
thonged whip. the throng follows the oxcart. dogma
and bondage, up from the fleet. john, the saints are
marching. god is queasied into life. at edgehill, or
at brentford. taken to the tower. stripped to the waist,
skinned illiterate. to shave a *martyr's* flesh against
the grain. noisy john, the saints are marching. onyx
eye, the hand, the brain. the slant unsound. and pale
lips twisted tight as a wet knot. a tooth is pulled; thin
mouths leaking their difficult creed. and puritan
souls are preened in the heat. vengeance, penitence,
regiments. later there will be *witches*, old women
kippered in smoke. their split skin spits a hot clear
fat like cider vinegar. the pyres are refining their
flames tonight. history is repeating. itself to itself.
with minor revisions. everything breaks. radial,
pinhole, hairline. everything breaks. court martials,
misdemeanours, mutinies. *honest john*, the saints
are staring, stir and crazed. foiled grief and rapt
folly. burford draws her complicated darkness
down in shame and wailing, veils and stones. god
is summoned like a duellist's second between
their vaulting lusts and vulgar songs. the head is
held between the hands. faith as an english malady.
faith in its many earnest perversions. a knife is
made a moth among the fabrics of a man.
professions and furies. professional fury. oracle
or prophet. the goblin logic of militias. utmost
unconditional red. leering and scheming. fusils
and nooses. honest, john, if you had seen. yellow
face they cradled, candled like an egg. america

turns toward you first. auspicious greed. meanwhile
i tried to love. bonny bess, thin filament of seaweed
grief. in green. *seventeen years of sorrows.*
seventeen! i tried to love. pictured though, what
hands had wrung, what hands had wrought.
those women's hands. not facet, but a diamond
fact. a greater love. your language leans
into its sneer. takes me apart. with axe or tract.

turning earth

i.m. Gerrard Winstanley

god holds us all in the hollow of his hand, costing
our melt-weight. from boy to man. stripling into
ingot. i see it now, we *are* more precious, we are
not less base. our swords, they are not morphing
into ploughshares, and every cutting blade insists
upon its own utopian intercourse. god is not *found*,
but *made*. these yeomen, apprentice lads. oh, we
have smithied *his* kingdom, reckoned it level with
hot, dull force. they call this *treason*. we'd turn
the stifled earth and let it breathe. the ground, not
broke, but opened after all. god holds us close.
they only see what we tear down. but god will
know, will know us for waywardens of the soil.
the soul. brothers, i dream of a spring without
omission, rising blue and green from winter's
cryptic jinx. sisters, i dream of a spring without
remission; a love that shrugs the slog of mongrel
toil. god holds, god knows. man is not made
for minting open mouths. man is not made for
driving stakes into the frozen ground. *they* skim
the fat, *we* till a trough of stones. man should
be held, man should be known by what he
grows: the shoot, the word, the human good.
we planted christ. came capsized and aspiring,
sweated our tenure in stockades, and stung
into hunger, ate grass. we planted christ. not
christ as a bright dividing line, but christ, an
immovable root that binds the chalky earth
together. crisis ripens a fist like a snail. we
rage and are imperfect, yet we know, we are
vouchsafed, and all are saved. for it is hope
that we make grow.

maschinenstürmer

of Ned Ludd, etc.

apocryphal captain, savant and stevedore, you
are a union man. ned ludd, you're lighting a last
dissenting cigarette, and holding the glowing tip
to my mind's eye. arch anachronist, you. ned
ludd, yours is the aspy temper, my toddler
brother's unreasoning rage. outlaw, *lone wolf*,
oh, the matinee swank of you. you're rainman
and andreas baader. saboteur, loose-hipped
autist, tightrope walker, gorgeous boy. you
orchestrate deformity, the world turned inside
out. ned ludd, you are the sweat of stockinged
faces, great train robberies, any horny crime.
messiah. crust-patch pariah. hot mess. syndrome
and spitting image, my bad girl's robin hood.
or no, you are splinters and misery; lecheries,
penury, mildewed futility. you're squared
needles and shallow graves. general of my
every swooning tendency. patron saint
of squatters. ned ludd, you beauty! foresaw
our hurt futures, streamlined by machines
to a passible ration. their rainbow's end is
rendered in soundproof glass, objectless
concrete, monoxide and chrome. ned ludd,
you saw our fathers scarping their pride
from their boots; the breadline's hollywood
blockbuster queue. men in whose lungs
a storm of metal shavings, babies riding
 like ships in bottles, swimming in foetal
alcohol. you, figment, you alone had named
this crabby, carpal doom. apocryphal captain,
eye patch and V mask, and a clipart sickle.

ned ludd, my militant poltergeist, i follow
your several extremes of haunting. ned ludd,
our whiskey priest, berserking his sermon in
a furious mood. ned ludd of the shut pit,
the lidless eye, the land torn out from under
us in some obscene white tablecloth trick.
ned, our ned, meaning meat-packing
laggard, the knackers yard, the common
cloth. the drones are wheeling like omen
birds; the failed assessments sleep six
to a mattress. ned, our invisible friend,
don't fail us now.

public lecture

"the purchasing power of agricultural wages was 40 per cent lower in 1570 than in 1450. As a result, it became impossible to support a household containing young children or infirm adults on wage labour..."

she says. i dream of martyrs' mischiefs. things
remote and then revealed: jack cade, quartered;
the poor commons of kent, routed and scoured.
fanatical attentions, folded-faces. you, hanging
listless in the pillory of a poorly pressed suit,
the airtight turmoil in my gut. give the century
its skirmishes, incite and license all collapse.
we coin new crisis hourly; ply our riot against
misrule, your catalogue of crowns. we are
stuck, sessile and assailed. i dream of ceded
fiefdoms, of precedents, repeals. our long, cold
night is sectioned into sieges, or the claims
of rival roses; your extraordinary distresses,
kent. your brutalist's warrant of chalk. this is
my dream: penury portending insurrection,
the lightly reckoned necks of vagrants
and of traitors. emaciated labour, leagues
and guilds. and men, syndicated bitterly,
execute routines: the hokey-cokey of execution,
execration, the tyrant's damp *alas*, the bigot's
sour *amen*. i dream a dream of righteousness,
riddled into writs, writ in a calfskin codex.
the pig who is stretched into vellum; the goose
plundered for primaries: scribal and flightless.
clerks, who fabricate feathers; informers,
foremen, forgers. i dream of wat tyler, tilling
the tax collector's head, the wrath of roseate
angels whose hour is at hand. kent, you are
slashed in the neck, paraded on pikes,

dragged like a plough behind horses. this
crew of skulled dunces, dancing. on hot
coals, on livid cinders of conscience. stop.
these are tiltyard retributions, tournaments
and courses, antics for ascension days. but we
will bury all errants, beneath the conjuries
of commonweal. their distorted law, and our
extinguished skin. kent, like a loafing ghost will
rise. cuckoos of the calendar. sing, dream. you
mendicants, you miscreants, you louts of rebel
decibel. give the populace its knives. bright
knaves. you plebs of brimstone and fidelity.

cade's chroniques

tight-lipped light tipped down toward
bank and fen, the yokeman's meadow.
sodden skies will tutor me to brood. yr
den of nettles, kent. the muddy bulge
and muddle of u. there is a little bird
that sits in scrub and sedge and sings
its hedge-invective. teach me this, yr
sparrow's gammon. sauntersick, i am,
and thistle-billeted. they scant yr right
of shack, and laugh to see yr manhood
thatched with spit and twigs. they call
u rabble kent, tap-shackled obstinates.
rascal kent, u rakes of affray. they call
u kent of mongrel measures, mulling
yr dull wits to malady; pot-plateaued
kent, whose livery is ditches. they do
not love u, mullocked sons of chalk. I
know. oh, u chronics of kent, hold me
up! they have their law, and it comes
in swinging its chancer's mallet. men
there are, who live to heap yr head
with conqueror's calumnies, a mean
encoffined logic under which we lean
like wheat. kent, they shall kill me. u,
must be free. in the vigour of yr sling-
shots. rēsen, rise. the brawny disarray
of u. blackthorn, cockspur, purging
buckthorn, quickthorn, firethorn, all
the thorns of thrusting fief. on yr hind-
legs through the wet hush. to file yr
teeth. tight-lipped light tipped down
toward the samphire bank where cade
has crept. will pierce the very varying
moon in its emphasising eye.

"And myscheff is nothyng redress"

tax and tallege, extortionate means.
handwork and husbandry, spoiled
and subdued. by feigned indictment,
false arrest. we were *legemene*. men
of pledge and siege. men of byre
and barrow, gatherers of samphire.
now recast as kin to kern, lubber-
fiends of felony, prodigies of lob.
you have wrought this change in
us. now we live by briar and bier.
you, amidst the self-made mire
of multiplying briberies. cade has
come a *wodewose*, the forest is
his throne. cade, and his clabbery
antic; scapeghost, whittled out
of roguery. *you* turn the jolly
drovers into diverse devils. *you*,
your *law*, the midden's *schrift*,
has driven us to wald and wold.
clench-penny pretender, tightening
your bible like a belt. while we,
slink into sheugh, apparelled in
scutch, in sedge and beggary,
knitbone, boneset. beset by knots
of bondage. we were *legemene*.
now, our names debased, we
come, stunted and punching,
hexing your wavering realm to
wreck with our pelting speech,
our slang of upstart arrows. we
come, shrapnelled by famine,
branded and bandying hazard.
cade as gallowglass, wanton

golidard, bloodshot cully, letting
blood. you wrought this change.
and we, bramble-backed subjects
of sod. we, hedge-haunters, head-
hunters, scalp-takers. we are upon
you, beseeching the heath. seething.
besieging. search and destroy.

a prophesy

time's up. put away your dusty bunting,
your breeks of cherished tweed. we'll
no more coppice kings to grow them
back at twice the strength. slough off
our fogey deference, the *tug* and *doff*
of monarchising forelocks, common
coifs, and caps of linen cloth. these we
cut, and burn. time's up. no more your
feints and fables; your parables are
bankrupt. and struck from roll or
warrant any record of your name.
time's gone, for drollery hours, sad
scholia and glosses, those legends
of heredity on which you stake your
claim. we were pollarding republics
while you slept. now we assert our
right to turbary and pannage. no
more *trespass against the vert*, no
more will your assart our common
forest, enclose with wattle hurdles
the thicket and the copse. time's up,
your golden names recede to spit
and shimmer on the tongue. we are
rising now, from scullery and gutter;
from doldrum, dungeon, drudge
and toil. we'll find you out, rise up
into your donjon. by *angstloch*
and by trapdoor. by fire, by phrase,
by torch and taper. blue touch paper.
ink and boiling oil.

lady chapel

...all images, relics, table-monuments of miracles, shrines, etc., be so totally demolished & obliterated with all speed & diligence that no remains or memory of them might be found for the future.
—thomas goodrich, 1541

virtue is a verbal art: *sophrosyne*, the crushed tongue treading
air between pincers. the mouth is hollow. its slow continence
of pain. how strict a chant to echo in the *chevet*, in the head, in
this scraping progress of pillars. lancet answers the lancet arch,
spandrels' gilded abscess cupped. then struck. the white stone
sighing its sinister modesty up. silence, my scenes and cycles.
to be a harem of weak needles, woundedly pointing. to break
the slender mortise of our effort: the mouth is hollow, excised
and sealed. pale curve to cradle the cancelled tendons of our
beseeching. gutted. cut all stiff expressions of harm. names
knocked into spur and stem. mason's mark, vandal's boast.
your ordinary's portent. through the chaste bracket of our
body you pass like asarum purge. the dumb sea empties
its tides. the dumb ship scuppers the stuttering fens.

æthelthryth

degree, decree, descent. yr castles and yr anarchies.
pivot and spit down yr dowry of stale crowns. to tilt
in my pilloried sleep, this hymn of buboes, fruiting
goitres, a farcical effort of cells. to limn my wanting
body into canons, into cantos, into all the prick-louse
absolutes of men. eternity is long. mine is the *contra-
naturam* that halts and dissolves yr power: the cord-
wood wincing into bloom, yr cup of tumult emptied.
what do u know? with yr *yas queen!* flying at half-
mast, yr riders of whale song and unicorn tears, with
yr lawful and tranquillised warbling. little world, u
settle for suffering, compress yr calendars of spleen
into sad frenzies of debt. u and yr morbid gallery
of wives, yr insular mission, yr cellar of dignified
heads. mine is the luminous insult of flesh unmade,
remade, returned. impossible body, corruption's
lean eclipse. no ribbons nor rosettes, no hawkers'
tawdries hold me. the black imagined habit u sable
me inside of. repulsed by gold, its needless solar
telegraph. to choose this pain as proper to the body.
to live within the grim ecstatic swim of it. my own
ultimatum. or god's. i wade the marsh, i chance
the tide. an estuary opens into me. u sink beneath
my nothing weight of seas.

our mother's day will come

i.m. Annie Kennedy (and also for our mother)

our mother's face exists in the space between
the *kaijū* and the *sphinx*. she's wearing clothes
that hold her body in contempt: green gingham
bib. her breath, imperfect peppermint. she has
to go *to work*. her crooked amulet earrings,
shorn of their funerary usage, palest flirtation
in dubious gold. unclaimed merest flick of skin,
the seldom-surfaced self. our mother *holds
down* several jobs, like righteous women said
to trample serpents underfoot. long shifts in
the kitchens of holiday parks, spiting her
wrists with ambergris and hot fat; salt to
the cut in her thumb. she works, waiting on
tables, while other people's children scream
with tactless joy, engineering ice-cream
headache, on and on. our mother's scanned
your hummocks of steroidal meat for hours,
her hands making a dumb-show out
of séance. small-talk and snide remark,
back pain and pricing error. again and again.
we heard her cry when she thought we were
asleep, a low drone like a fly trapped in
an airless room. our mother worked lates
with the cold coiled inside like a sharpened
spring at the twenty-four seven garage too
tight to pay for heat. she gritted her teeth
through gregarious sleaze in the small town
slur of the local bar. scraped back hair
and scrimping, she came home and kneaded
bread, like she was thumping life back into
a cardiac case. she held us, through all our

recalcitrant havoc, the voices we heard in
our heads between god and the vomit, our
gremlins and lurgies and rages. our mother
studied. in those hotbed-of-non-event towns,
she dug in her heels, and she bit back her
anger. not *a shoulder to cry on*, a human
shield, her backbone a needle of lightning.
she studied, defended, and cleaned on her
knees till she bruised. my mother, our
mother, unfolding the joke from a book
that the world had kept from her. our
mother, coming sudden on the mind's
reckless hieroglyphs: *i finally understand*.
mellow fruitfulness, molly bloom, emma
goldman, sylvia plath. my mother's face
exists between the strange and the wise.
and we catch her sometimes, when she's
only herself, dreaming her private tumult.
my mother works, tilling the stony earth
until a word strikes water and everything
wickedly greens for a moment. and this is
the grace that shit is grist to. it is thanks
to her we are all of us free.

cable street 1936/ 1981

for all those who fight fascism, wherever it rears its ugly head

the uniforms were flocking. we would not let them pass.
there was broken glass in the treads of our second-hand
shoes. 81 was more of the same: cirrhosis, dopamine,
the national front in hobnail squadrons out on some brutalist
errand or other; millwall, post-industrial doldrums, passing
a hat at the galtymore. the mood was casual delinquency,
upward mobility, the absence of god. black shirts like comic
vampires. a picket line and a prison riot, a diplock court,
a brick through the window. and you, borstal boy, absconding
from a hospital. *where are you going?* and *where are you from?*
the questions don't change. the tv beaming lip-synch
and static. beaded seat covers and scented candles. latex
and lube and pedantic erotica, soho and camden. kilburn market
is a lion tamer's cage. roubles and whooping cough. scruple
and impeded speech. spg, *by cruelties caused*. the north, flexing
its rhetoric, seismic, stricken and running interference. *oi, gyp!
oi, yid! you paki caant!* we heard it all. the dogshit breath
of letterboxes, poltergeist activity, the artifice of occupation.
no one saw and no one sees. hire purchase, right to buy.
and other such thatcherite wheezes. the hospital. maggie,
beatific in tantrum, face of a hanging judge: *we will not
negotiate with terrorists.* neither will we, no matter their
rank or badge number. antipathy, video nastiness, satellites,
satanic panic; bigots with no inside voice. long kesh, and all
the chivalries of wasting sickness. my mother singing
and lilies on the window ledge. fear, queering the breath
in our lungs. cover our faces and holding our breath.
home for the holidays, green defeatist air we sucked
the merest smoke of. smirking grace. beautiful boys,
peacocked and plummeting. this year's look: men,
on their knees, one earring in, down to their last

agonised recourse. we're heading for orgreave
and the algarve, for cancer and for clubland, fanatical
tenderness. ideation over unemployment blackspots.
house arrest. metropolitan nutjobs in bavarian headgear
and horsebrass. a rome where all roads lead. sus.
cracked ribs in brixton instrumental. *babylon*. anti-nazi
calisthenics: cringe and stretch *protecting his head with
my arms*, you said. we ran away, we ran to ground.
to *stomping ground*. the vegetarian peasantry, driven
from the land, lifting their dreads like snake handlers.
bewilderment and welcome break. silence. incapable,
occluded, chewing wasps, sucking piss off a thc treated
thistle. *dirty squatters*, eco-warriors. worrisome
sanctuary. home-schooled and under investigation:
you don't look like much of a warrior to me. need
money. need treatment. galleoned in call centres,
quaking. persons unknown. passive aggressive
skincare ritual. *i cut my hair. am i beautiful now?* it is
more of the same. vested interests, tempted fates.
our history, you said. gilded and devoured by turns.
ten black t-shirts on a line outside dial house.
it was the best of times. scratch that. they will not
pass. even now, they will not pass. pick the pages
free of broken glass.

news from nowhere

i.m. William Morris

prisons, indeed! and i stand on the hill without
threat or incentive, facing the light. once, we
were free, but by-laws and bailiffs, ambition's
brass neck, these things brought us low. please
bear this in mind: morris spoke, and his fables
graced us. once, we believed. then money come,
our skinny green disease. soliciting malignancy,
from chalk farm to saint paul's. oh, there used
to be trees. chickweed and reeds, the river's
silvery guesswork; silence and space. god's
speed was a slow proposal, foliate, and growing.
we used to be free. we leant them a hand, they
folded our fingers over a ten-bob note. thames
is a fist of tidal filth. there is a hole in our boat.

great escapists

for the "gay traitors", known and unknown

to stand where you stood, and to cradle my culpable
love. no passive phantom, you, but everywhere a red
intruding star. wayward boy, i'm on your side. blatant
and fallible, discomposed. but that's what loving does.
these stones command obedience, or else inspire
a more complete devotion. there are still those who
do not know the difference. but don't lose heart. boy,
on the burning deck. shrug dogma and indoctrination
both. give them the slip, those honey-mouthed mothers
of melo, all. you were not wrong. instructive human
wreck. truculent, encumbered; disordered and entwined.
but i'd not swap your fraught and transfixed creed for
all their drawling hibernative talk of *loyalty*. to stand
where you once stood: the colleges gird their impossible
lawns. protect the past, the inching pace of change. do
not lose heart, you were not wrong. we are all pawns
your solemn folly, mistaken trust. but still the *dream*
was sound. i know the pain you're radiant and sodden
with. oh busy, awkward ghost, please cut yourself
some slack. i stand where you once stood, and looking
in, not looking back, feeling the fond shock of a heart's
belonging. one day this will be ours: the spectacle,
the reverie, the flowers, sharpening their leaves against
the wet edge of the spring. all good things: a straight
back and sense of worth. it's possible. you were so right.

Cambridge, 2018/ 2023

#2

tonight, cheam is the dry white taste of selective blessings.
i learn about your house for the first time, now that only
the garden remains, a reeking vernal hinterland where
foxes preside in exile over heaps of small bones. headless
sparrows, rats, the casualties of native cunning. unsprung
swingsets sag. did you miss this life, i wonder? made your
bed, an in-law said, then called you wicked. i'd beg to differ.
i see you feeding a fox from your hand. the way you shrugged
and shied from every craving they made staple of. *never
aspire at another's expense. never confess. soft hearts need
stern natures.* this, i know. did your falter? in the flipped
image, discover yourself diminished in the act of doubling?
gentle pedant, you had the world, they will never forgive.
could steer from the plushy cockpit of a private club,
the whole wide rolling thing. you wanted less. meticulous
illusionaire. we, who have clung to our rifles and shrines,
concocted clumsy lusts against despair; we who have gone
hungry and unwashed, whose *home* is a slurred denial
of pride, salute you as is due. we hop the fence on our
way home; scatter flowers and think of you.

Hampstead / Cheam, 2018

on fighting on

i cannot kiss this better; retrieve a token bliss
from broken teeth, on friday night or otherwise.
i know that now. they make incessant fetish
from the vegetative english dead; you don't
belong. *fuck off!* they said. i cannot kiss this
better; the old accused and clouded heart.
you're fit enough. they sent a letter, spread
a sad, mutating shame; your hijacked mind
was reeling and your pockets full of stones.
i cannot make this better. the children stew
in uniforms, and take instruction in a sneer.
the ethic of their ignorance, a stifled pride
they daub on walls or break a window with.
there's nothing better left round here.
i cannot make this better. the paper sprouts
opinions, promiscuous as weeds. we are
the *undeserving poor*, so televise our erring
faces, slurring in a sound bite. a viral slight
they slip between the ribs; a smile that serves
to show the teeth, distorts the jaw. i cannot
kiss this better, the rifle butt to your mother's
chin; the door the bawling troops kicked in,
the hank of hair they tore out at the roots;
a conscience polished for parades, the armour
of their accolades, our blood and muck still
clinging to their boots. and all throughout
the politicians smirk, upholstered in their
pedigree. and people, drunk on lapis sap,
applaud the spoilt heredity of windsors;
their balconies are panting with long tongues
of ugly bunting. i cannot kiss this better.
nobody can fight alone nostalgia's analgesic
trap. but we can work together. we are still

here—we can, we must—rebuild again in faith
and trust. this land is *ours*, we want it back.

fleet

the witch collects animal bones along the bank of the thames

this is after our first bright erring: coffee, and a frilly
light across the thames. the men i met had two moods,
the profligate, the flagellant. i wanted better grace; to
feed this something unappeased and inward. i am so
tired of poets, that choir of consummate brains. i am
so tired. i need the tide's beseeching suck, to scuff
or tear the sole of my misshapen life against a pebble
bed, the river's shardy, mardy, muddy lip. i've always
known that love is either *coaxed* or *wrenched*. but
was my best affection tricked or torn? now, there is
the old cloth merchant's rub. *baksheesh*, a satin sheet,
an index finger grubbing round its rosy thumb.
to *reckon*, to *erase*. these meanings hug themselves
like unloved children. i am chancing backward down
a ladder to the twisted ankle, spectre, skelf, and sherd.
above is *wedge of lemon*, a lispy breeze buffooning
in a blonde crop; is bubble-busking, cover versions,
burning sugar, living statues, every strutting thing.
here is where the river feeds the river with the river;
where my unlovely thames enriches her defeatist
whisper. all the choicest filth from down a hoodlum
fleet: the cobalt wrecks of stencilled ships, the lintels
of bedsitting rooms; discarded cockney scoff in
shape of oyster shells like heavy plates of leadblue
medieval armour. wharf and quay. man and boy.
an abattoir's circus tumble. painted majolica,
chophouse pottery. the champed bits of a clay pipe.
here is a lost commonwealth of bone, femurs
bronzed and sharp, my *arrows of desire*. this pill
bottle is a glass green lazarus, rising cool amidst
an animal armada. strata. pedigree. a mastiff rib is

a scimitar. a shoulder spirals inward like a shell.
black vertebrae, an anglian crown. i gather these
in, trace their porous geographies, prize them for
their defects. this is after our first bright erring:
end of the day, a sallow, depthless sky. bone,
be my jagged familiar, connect me to a rightful
world, before i tilt, and drift, or sink. before i hug
the level depths like so much plundered coin.

the travesties

i

in the tedious suction of summer i'm squat
beside the inoperable dog and picking at food;
the news is fat with travesty, soft woe that boils
the bones for soup, the usual: brown child lies
on its side in the dirt like a grubby cutlet. viral
child extends its face towards the fold-away
couch. we've seen this before, we're old, we
dream of pristine beaches. look, i am setting
the scene: sunday night, and in an inky mood,
we watch tv. climate denial, the grunting
science we make prayer to. *democracy does
not work!* and we are sutton's antifa, bastion
and exhausted, we can't save anyone. i am
afraid. how famine happens like a scream in
a staring match, how famine happens
like a horse in a storm. and famine could
happen to anyone. we watch tv. africa,
her eye teeth are gold. romania retrieves
her lullabies from ditches. *a week in politics
is a long time!* we have no real appetite to
speak of, scraping the glaze from our plates,
say *here, you wash, i'll dry*, and chore becomes
devotion too. there's nothing else. i cannot
drag my breath into beautiful pleading; i dither
my hands, petting a small black pan, this
witches' familiar. outside there is only the war,
eight hundred years of rust and thirst; their nails
and chambers; galley bondage, *kesseltreiben*.
and now the slowly soldiering worm, his piqued
dominion. *deprivation is relative*, and anyway,
we will all die screaming, walking backwards
into the sea, lying cables of blood from our
soft monkey eyes. we watch tv. my throat
vibrates to a loadbearing sigh.

ii

the sky is pink and ticklish with fatigue; the heat
settles in stiff pleats, a corrugated light ironing
creases into the scurvy dusk. around the ground
floor flats behind the gasworks the grass is yellow
chalk to touch, and several smutty tabbies rake
their low-slung slouching bellies along the hot
rails of an evening. bull breeds pant on piebald
scrub, the verges dirt, berserk with daisies. oh,
endless summer, encore end of day that doesn't
end. late blooming boys sweat milk; thin girls
willowed on tryptamine, dancing, their flashing
nails delight dilated eyes. in bedrooms, braced
for vespertine debasements, the young offenders
lisp themselves awake. we shall begin, we are
all beginning, beginning again. in the pub on
the corner you drink sunlight into sawdust, your
kisses into kites. south of the river, and she has
forgotten more than she ever knew; has turned her
sentry faces to the wall: smote brick and banishment;
diesel fumes, her dubious pheromone. and now
the glandular parks are running a fever; communal
breath like swimming baths, the pigeon chests
of children, strays, crazed magpies, and the cauliflower
faces of veterans. exhale. a ghost flows into
your held breath, and where is poetry? that laughable
science that lives in the eye. it is lost to the damp
rapport of roundshaw and belmont: pushbike boys
selling wet meat in carparks and gardens; a taste
of re-fried styrofoam, or a limp rummage of prawns.
citizen pit bull with amber eyes is scavenging scraps.
the sniffed crotch itching in jeggings on benches.
we eat and eat. these thin vinegar wings grating
the tongue, all shard and fossil, impossibly heimlich.

soapy beer, our weak tisane, the brew we wade
like baptists. oh, to eat the rubbery guts of horses,
to teethe an ancient wedge of lemon; to wipe
ourselves, perspire our common poisons, like grey
halal kebabs

iii

this corner merits a dog, a fox, a drunk in
a garbled park. i've nothing worth stealing.
urban dejection, the fat cheque you renege
on, and these borough churches bode no
rapture. cashed and carried away with
ourselves. i'm sucking on sherbet, sweetest
tooth in a temperance bar. we're latex,
pox and glamorama. everyone mogul
and vintage and spree. anonymous
coffee, generic pop-up. pink meringues
like periwigs. we're here for the shellac,
the rag trade; the obsolete linings of suits.
that's charity! the real hip scrimp of us!
it's getting late. jalfrezi and meth, refried
gold and *taste the fucking rainbow*.
taxies are nosing like moles
into the town centre, with its bashable
skulls and strange protocols of decay.
our sunburn is become a uniform.
beerguts fly their football shirts at half-
mast. chelsea at home. christ, give me
somewhere my cramped desire can
breathe, not this, proud circus, burnt in
matinee arson bright; the kitten heels
they kick from under us like crutches.
anywhere but here: crack daddies
imploring, pilgrims suffering south.
morden, merton, the saturday chancers
whose church is a stark khazi, a stolen
phone; whose religious life is fluke
and certitude, penny-ante aggrogasm.
anywhere at all: sky as white as
nuclear comeuppance. the beautified

faces of perfume-counter girls all
drawing a blank. the landlord's torso,
mauve in an indecisive light; a *butchers'
dozen* of stupid boys, blenched, stretchered,
the casualties of grim recreation. new
addington, a&e, collateral palace.
ragged in scant asylum, nurses
equipped for belligerent triage,
for third degree burns, epilepsy
and languishing, congenital hell.
we are not the worst, but the women
round here have hollow bones,
and a small dog twitches on
a nylon lead like a teased prick. no,
we are not the worst, we have
the weekend, its sly mediocrity
and minor violence. we are
the bludgeon poor, lionised
and advertised at; overcrowded,
cretinous, and the heart gapes in
its rubble like a sink in a cleared
slum. we are here. we are always here.
for the bodycon, bitches, the headcanon
slang of obsessive youth, drunk phantoms
swirling their shadows like opera capes. we
are here; in lycra and nikes we hesitate
skyward on mildewed wings. it is
evening, a blizzard of frail colour works
itself to earth. sutton, an arcade game
glow round her, ventures a halo.
let light pollution pall into
your open mouth. look up, where
god is floating like a suicide blonde
in a bathtub; a turd in the firmament.

iv

lover, they hate us, whose poverty is gnawed
affront, whose poverty performs this rotten city
rotten. i'm rocking this blue mood, this mooning
lust, this crumpled housecoat. i make my pelvic
thrusts against the tall buildings, with their lowering
missionary emphasis. i have pink spit and pitiful
brilliance. you can buy a good time, you can see
up my skirt.

lover, they hate us, whose lore is halcyon
faltering; hate, for the drunk, low forage
of living; the squeaky dread that fills
us up like helium, end of the month, with
bailiffs shaking industrious daggers. i'm
the literal worst. and you. the flaunting
poor who live by binge and famine; bestial
trending, sex-texting girls, stocious, stacked,
such cairns of teetering flesh.

lover, they loathe the brittle romance
of skirmish; how we twist to lip at dregs
of brash delight, unzipping in the multiplex,
beneath the septic light of bowling alleys.
they hate us, who grieve in scutty flourish;
dead-end genomes, excelled at sentimental
dereliction, trinket kisses tumbled from
the argos catalogue. lover, for our default
denims, for the soused vowel; for the mind's
eye, styling a storm.

lover, we are the caterwaul culpable poor,
and we shall never sally free. our faces
franked for blank jeering, flapping a scream
like an empty sleeve.

v

outside the station the christian scientists have banded
together, caught in an act of forlorn witness. jesus, a ranting
pneumatic hippy, thunders towards them like a bus without
breaks. the air crackles, full of canned laughter and amphetamine
psychosis, and the rosehill women go by, white knuckling
reusable carrier bags. they cover their hair, they are lovely,
their sleeves billow like wings. it is eid, in its fervent banter
and breaking fasts. *a time for peace*, a small child says.
his love is toy and he is lucky. in the north they mobilise
their dour festivities without me. i dream of a beautiful boy
laid out in his bower of petrol station baby's breath, as still
as a slaughtered faun. i do not belong here. i belong to
the quivering dark-eyed unction of priests, slim boys, bearded,
rolling out their beta-tested faith from jesuit colleges. i do not
belong here. i am alone, and it is terrible: day after day, minting
my undermined thoughts in a small font sadly, unable to solve
the twice-shy rocket science of self, the body, its omnidirectional
blossoming. i am alone with my misdirected flesh, a wasting
war i've fought in inches. my father's face, hung in my life
like the sun, all *what have you done, girl,* and *where are you
going?* he burns with the same extrovert indifference as stars.
violet fire than jars the sight. that's exile, a distance measured
in units of shame. i do not belong here. and michael most i
dream of you. i dream of saints, their wild travail of dances.
wran jag. stag mask. michael, i dream of you. let this be
an intercession: god, in his white gloves, his coy magic
an infinite triage. you are *saint* michael and you are an angel;
you have the black tongue of a sparrow. i am unworthy,
i am from dirt, i am unclean, my appetite whetted for wounds.
i cannot love, but i stagger in my raptures like the sea.
michael, your song is siren, siphon, it pours my pulse out
of me. your flight is a wedding feast. fifteen weeks of living
off light and your teeth are talismans, michael. your black

tongue is a whelk, is a worm, is wooing the shell-like sanctum
of my inner ear. you are naked, your nakedness is pious
chainmail. you are a phoenix, your nakedness raves. i am
stained with tormentil and tansy. i pick potent leaves
from the scrub behind the houses. my love is a landfill,
the seagulls spirit my soul above carshalton pond. i do not
belong. i am an unclean thing, but i long to come to you,
diligent and mended, caustic-clean, as bleached as a bed
somebody has died in. i am not mad. it is the season for religious
audacities, for fireworks, pledges, the intemperate evangelism
of corner boys. it is the season for god, saturate, steroidal,
glassy-eyed in the token gold of pawn brokers' windows.
oh, but this is an edible god, a smokeable god, a god of ganja
and linseed. mine is the moaned god, whose coming is stupefied
pavane. in sutton, only the mad have heard my god. belmont,
and the quaint punishments of a half-way house, they know
my god. elephant and castle, a rome where all roads lead,
they have seen my god. my god is a god of graft and starlings.
host. a tender murmuration, and you are his right hand, stood
at his shoulder like a silent minder. michael, it is you. an alarm
is peeled from the moist mouth of the evening. a burning building
is equal to my utter lack of fucking surprise. the face of god
is a riot, fragments of glass, and mighty in sorrow. our local
member is out and about, grinning like a school bully, shaking
his soul in his hands like a nine-sided dice. *we know what to do
about that, girl.* no. not here. where the buses idle the air
is a gruel of fumes and nothing grows. you are saint michael
and you are an angel. your name resounds like a joy ride,
the whooping bark of dogs. i have loved you. and here
i am, nursing my own particular banishment. the free sheet
waxes anarchy and ethnic tantrum. the pharmacy window, green
with anatomical gashes; the ring road is a tide mark on a narrow,
nasty bath. we will never come clean. a girl in a head scarf is pertly
spiritual; she has tiny black shoes like poor church mice, her patent
leather squeaks. her body frets in and out of shape and you are

a warm light that lifts the face in laughing. all the fried chicken
shops along the one way system are billowing incense.
a perfect circle is a church. and sutton is a circle too.

Notes on the poems

'**witchfinder's cabaret**' is a poem about, and born from, shock. More accurately, it is a poem about the ways in which we experience and encounter our own history as a succession of rude awakenings: the first shock being that people in the past could persecute and brutalise each other with such inventiveness and zeal, the second shock being that one's ideological "enemies" do not possess the monopoly on wanton cruelty, and the third and most sustaining shock being the myriad resurgences and survivals of this cruelty in the present.

The poem was sparked by a news item about a proposed memorial to the eight women put to death as the "Witches of Islandmagee" in Carrickfergus in 1711. A TUV councillor, Jack McKee, objected to the memorial as "anti-God" and a potential "shrine to paganism". Yep. Genuinely. The story provoked a deep period of reflection in me about our selective memories, as communities and individuals, and our tendency to fetishize the parts of the past that cast us as either heroes or victims. The truth is far more complicated, and the long history of religious terror in England and the North of Ireland has distributed its atrocities fairly evenly between Catholics and Protestants, Monarchists and Republicans. It still does.

'**you ask us why we fight**' was written in honour of, and partially channelling the voice of, the Chartist leader Fergus O'Connor (1796-1855). More than this, it's a poem that attempts to pick apart his characterisation in a lot of the literature I encountered when trying to probe his legend a little deeper. O'Connor's commitment towards the use of physical force in the furtherance of his radical agenda, and his open hostility towards the methods of other Chartist leaders such as William Lovette and Henry Vincent, split the movement. O'Connor was certainly an erratic and divisive figure, and many have argued that his destabilising influence and frequent rhetorical outbursts massively undermined the credibility of the Chartist cause. Arrested on numerous occasions for the assault on several other MPs, O'Connor was ultimately declared insane and committed to the asylum at Chiswick where he died. O'Connor's portrayal, however, as violent and egomaniacal, ignores the righteousness of his anger, the brute desperation of the times, and the corrosive effect on the soul of the struggle to live with dignity and justice. In O'Connor's commitment to physical force I read both ideological and emotional echoes in my own communities. Violence might not be "the answer", but for all our hand-wringing squeamishness about this particular brand of direct action, it erupts from a well of anguished experience, exhaustion and despair that has no better form of redress. I have often wondered how people can condemn the violence of individuals while seeming to accept the greater systemic violence that hedges the lives of those individuals at every turn. Progress by moral force is slow, and to place an expectation of patience on the backs of those already unimaginably overburdened by threat, precarity and poverty, appears to me to be singularly unjust. That isn't to "condone" violence, but to make some effort to understand what drives it, to look on those who perpetrate it with at least partial sympathy.

'**noisy john**', also Freeborn John, Honest John, or plain old John Lilburne (1614-1657) was a political Leveller both before and during the English Revolution. The poem takes incidents from his life: his agitation for "freeborn rights", his imprisonment, exile, betrayal by Cromwell, and the violence visited upon him; tries (and fails) to sift the historical person from his various myths. Lilburne is a figure whose legend loomed large in the crusty-punk and traveller cohorts to which I belonged as a teenager and young adult. I knew him first through the music of bands like Blyth Power, The Levellers, and New Model Army, where he assumed the status of a radical mascot, a name to rally round. But the more you dig, the more you know, and although Lilburne was on the side of right, certainly more so than Oliver Cromwell, his message was liberal and libertarian, not truly radical; his "freeborn rights" were predicated on the ownership and protection of private property, not—as in the case of Winstanley and the Diggers—on its abolition. Perhaps Lilburne's greatest legacy is that his trial in 1641 has been credited as the foundation for the Fifth Amendment to the United States Constitution, an amendment that has provided legal protection to generations of demonstrators and activists. Lilburne's libertarian thinking has, in general, an unusual amount of traction in the States, which inflects his figure with ambivalence for someone like myself, a "Digger" in my sympathies, and ancestrally Catholic. The poem is about the contested ownership of historical figures and their legends, about the imaginative sway of Lilburne's myth over my own protest cohort.

'**turning earth**' is written in memory of Gerrard Winstanley (1609-1676) and the True Levellers or Diggers. I came to Winstanley through Green Anarchist (in one of its less Unabomber-enthusiastic iterations) during the 90s, and felt an instant affinity for his belief in common property, and the Diggers' radical direct action against the unjust encroachments of enclosure: tearing down fences, occupying land, planting seeds.

Growing up in the country the unfairness of enclosure, and other such elitist land grabs felt far closer, historically, and far more pertinent than they might have done had I spent my childhood in the city, or in suburbia. To look at the countryside today is to see the repercussions of the Enclosures Act and its lasting impact on the environment. In Winstanley, I found the ideological counterpart to the poetry of my favourite writer, John Clare, and the influence of both was profoundly felt throughout various squatter and traveller movements.

What I also wanted the poem to convey was a sense of faith as a liberating, galvanizing force. There's a tendency on the Left, in the West, to dismiss or revile belief as nothing but a dupe to the deluded, a con practiced against the unwary, an instrument of oppression. This approach is patronising, lacks nuance, and ignores the realities of people's lives while selectively editing the role of religious conviction, and of religious movements in shaping the rich and various histories of dissent. I'm very interested in liberation theology, and the radical potential of Christianity as interpreted by Winstanley and the Diggers, and so the poem channels religion as a positive and sustaining force. This hasn't always been my own experience, but I still believe it might be possible.

'**maschinenstürmer**' or "machine storm" is written out of my lifelong fascination with the apocryphal figure of Ned Ludd, a fascination that has been with me ever since a history teacher (one of the good ones) jokingly referred to me as a "Luddite" for my angry agrarianism (I was an insufferably earnest pre-teen). At first I took this comment as an insult. I'd heard the phrase before, used to confer lumpen, technologically illiterate status on its intended target, and I'd never really thought about where it came from. On the urging of my teacher I looked it up, and found a host of movements across Europe, not anti-progressive, but demanding a better definition of "progress" than that which sacrifices the lives of people on the altar of money.

The machines themselves weren't the point. It was, has always been, the rejection of a reckless and relentless profit motive. What struck me then, and strikes me still, is the way the word "Luddite" entered the lexicon, not as a marker, but as an erasure of working-class history. In its insulting inflection, in everything it came to stand for, there is a disavowal of our bravery, complexity, creativity and suffering. The poem posits a reinvigoration of this symbolic figure, and with it a reawakening to our own capacity for dissent.

'**public lecture**', '**cade's chroniques**', '**"and myscheff is nothyng redress"**' and '**a prophesy**' are a suite of poems concerned with the figure of Jack Cade and the Cade Rebellion of 1450. My interest in Cade was sparked by my move to Kent from South London three years ago, and these pieces are recent additions to the collection. While Cade's rebellion was arguably one of the most important popular uprisings to take place in England during the

Long Middle Ages, solid reliable information about Cade himself was—is—fairly thin on the ground.

During my research I encountered a similar propaganda effort as with the figure of Fergus O'Connor: Cade's rebelliousness is repeatedly located in an egomaniacal or irrational character, and a native predisposition to violence. Cade is often referred to as being of Irish decent, with Irishness and Kentishness being confused and conflated; used almost synonymously as a figure for negative civility. I've been really interested in how Cade's legend can be restored or reinvigorated to provide a people's history of Kent freed from the racist baggage of popular nationalistic scripts.

'**lady chapel**' refers to the Lady Chapel at Ely Cathedral, which was largely destroyed in the sixteenth century during the Reformation, where—in accordance with Puritan convictions—all forms of religious decoration were rejected and forcibly, violently erased. I was fascinated by the Chapel, and by the way in which the highly visible scars of its desecration become another kind of devotional mark; how the irrepressible spirit of its prior existence haunts the space Puritan forces sought to purge.

'**æthelthryth**' is another poem inspired by my visits to Ely Cathedral. Also known as Etheldreda, she was born around 636, a daughter of King Anna of East Anglia, married off twice for political reasons. As Queen she founded the abbey at Ely. Her legend states that she remained a virgin throughout both her marriages, and around 673 was finally released from her vows to become a nun, returning to Ely to found a double monastery for monks and nuns. I was inspired by the elements of her story that saw her negotiate and circumvent male power to accomplish astonishing things. While history tends to paint a fairly grim carceral picture of devotional service for women, Etheldreda was a spiritually and politically vigorous force to be reckoned with; her version of the renunciate life was one of principled vigilance, challenge, and escapist potential.

'**our mother's day will come**' was originally written for International Working Women's Day, and in it I try to honour the unsung, unlovable labours of working-class women, through the example of my own mother, but also calling on the ghosts of her/ our inspirational foresisters past. I wrote this poem not only to try and do some justice to a person whose doggedness and uncompromising militancy I greatly admire, but to make space for a story about women's labour, and about the struggle (in terms of money, in terms of expectations, in terms of time, in terms of sheer fatigue) of those women to raise consciousness and to contribute meaningfully to revolutionary work.

This is still something of an obsession for me. I wanted to reflect upon the myriad ways in which the dissenting histories of women have been censored and obscured; their commitment and profound contribution to radical social change omitted from our popular narratives of global struggle, and erased over time. Do the names Janie Terrero, Annie Kenny or Patricia Lynch mean anything to you? If not, you are not alone, and you are not to blame. Even in the most publicly accessible story of women's activism, that of the women's suffrage movement, so many voices have been lost or elided, edited out in order to create an acceptable version of this once incendiary campaign, a version that the capitalist patriarchy will tolerate: liberal, not militant; reformist, not revolutionary, and overwhelmingly middle class.

But working-class women were the life blood of that movement, and the uneasy relationship between their labour and their revolutionary activities is so illuminating about the ways in which work (which includes, but is not limited to, child bearing, child rearing and domestic labour) has been used to coerce, control, intimidate and oppress working-class women and women in poverty for centuries.

'cable street 1936/ 1981' has had many iterations, and grew out of what I've come to describe as an unofficial oral history project, listening to generations of antifascist activists, protestors, squatters, travellers and alternative communities talk about their long histories and experiences of resistance. The Battle of Cable Street has been described as the most popular antifascist battle ever to take place on British soil. It happened on the 4th of October 1936, when the working-class, largely Jewish community of East London successfully blocked the streets where they lived to prevent Oswald Mosley and his British Union of Fascists marching through.

I'd heard of Cable Street growing up, mainly through the song 'Ghosts of Cable Street' by The Men They Couldn't Hang, and one of my first self-imposed missions on coming to London was to get lost trying to find the place where this decisive battle occurred. The poem is less about the battle itself than its long legacy within anti-fascist and protest cohorts. Cable Street functions as both a beacon of exemplary radical action to future generations, and a grim reminder that history repeats, that fascism is like London's own Frankenstein's monster, lurching back to life at sporadic intervals, leaving trails of destruction and misery in its wake. The ending to this piece was revised following the fascist attack on Bookmarx on Saturday 4th August, 2018. Through those last lines I am trying to connect the frustrations, failures and moments of triumph in anti-fascist struggle throughout the thirties, the eighties, and into the present day.

'**news from nowhere**' is the shortest poem in this collection, but in some ways was the hardest to write. William Morris (1834-1896) was a designer, poet, novelist, translator, and socialist activist, whose utopian novel *News from Nowhere* had an enormous influence on New Age Traveller and self-styled alternative and eco-warrior communities during the nineties. I wanted to write something that honoured the beauty of Morris' dream while acknowledging the failures and disillusionments of those movements and individuals, my own included. I also wanted to inflect the poem with hope, the hope that although one generation has been co-opted, crushed, or has given in, there's a seed of possibility that so long as the river flows and Morris' words and dreams survive, a better world is still possible.

'**great escapists #1-2**' were written for and loosely about the so-called "Gay Traitors" or Cambridge Spies: Guy Burgess, Kim Philby, Anthony Blunt and Donald Maclean, focussing mainly on Burgess and Philby, figures for whom I have felt an abiding fascination since early adolescence. For people who had such inherited advantages to "betray" those advantages in the name of revolutionary communism was something quite startling to me; it messed with my sense of what revolutionary work looked like, the kinds of sacrifice it demanded of people. So this poem isn't a poem about working-class radicals, but the influence and imaginative legacy of these ambiguous figures on my own class-consciousness.

Burgess, Philby, Blunt and Maclean remain so interesting to us because they complicate our ideas about class struggle; ask us difficult questions about our own often troubled allegiances, and communism's often fraught past. The poems were written after visiting various Cambridge Spy-related landmarks (sometimes openly, sometimes covertly), and thinking about the divided loyalties and difficult histories invoked by the word "communism". My return to Cambridge as an unlikely Fellow/ interloper in 2022, granted (by no means easy) access to its cloistered spaces, sent me back to this poem, and had me thinking again about the energy and commitment required to penetrate its membrane of moneyed privilege; to think outside of that suffocating circle.

'**on fighting on**' draws on a few things, chiefly on the day-to-day difficulties of maintaining any sense of class solidarity in the face of bigotry, ignorance, threat, violence and cruelty. To think in those terms is hard, especially when the people you're supposed to feel solidarity with don't want you living next door to them; when they consistently vote for those who would dismantle your shared communities, destroy your livelihoods and remove your access to essential services. This sense of frustration goes double when thinking about Traveller communities, and as an antidote to that the poem takes courage from and inspiration in those acts of community defiance that bind us together against those who would oppress us. When I came to edit this poem, I was thinking particularly of Dale Farm, but I'm really talking about any moment working-class people come together and coalesce around the notion of resistance. One of the most maddening things for me in recent years has been the steady destruction of the opportunity for people in poverty to educate themselves. Rises in fees, cuts to basic maintenance and support, the closure of libraries, all this acts in concert to prevent people in poverty from accessing knowledge, inside the system of out of it. Our ability to opt out of the current educational establishment has also been severely curtailed, in tandem with changes to the National Curriculum that minimise the development of critical thinking.

In this climate it becomes increasingly difficult to evolve or maintain any kind of meaningful analytical faculty, and an insane amount of unequal effort to participate in education or academia at all. This is strategic and deliberate, and it needs acknowledging and fighting at every opportunity. This poem is my favourite in the collection because it offers the possibility of hope; hope that the world can be better, that people are capable of better effort. Not all of them, obviously, some people are just massive, massive dicks, but some, enough, more than we think. What socialism stands for, what it *should* stand for, is allowing people the possibility of growth, the potential for change. We deserve better. We can be better.

'fleet' is a kind of record of my own artistic and poetic practice, one which also serves as a metaphor for uncovering our collective histories. It records a day spent gathering animal bones and bits of crock and clay pipe from the banks of the Thames at the point where the older, subterranean waters of the Fleet feed into it, a point at which the detritus of centuries becomes the archive and the evidence of the present. There is something that piqued me, poetically, about this process: that the iconic Thames, girded by gilded glass shrines to wealth on either side, is nevertheless fed by darker, more subversive currents, bringing with them the clutter and debris of everyday life, and rendering this quotidian chaos suddenly visible, thanks to the rising tide. Our own histories surface in such ways, exposed at odd moments, opportunistic or accidental, and if we are attentive in such moments we catch their beauty and their strangeness, and a fleeting glimpse of figures not so unlike ourselves.

Notes on the travesties

To live "on the margins" is a geographical, political, and psychological condition, a condition in which it is not always easy to separate the scars of place from those of psyche. This, if anything, is what **the travesties** was about.

At the time of writing, I was asked to what "travesties" I was referring. The person asking this question had never been poor, had never experienced mental health problems, and had never been stuck in a scutty borough of South London. I feel for those who are able to fulfil any of the aforementioned criteria, the poem's title is fairly self-explanatory. Or perhaps it is not? Is the travesty that people live like this? Are the incidents and experiences of working-class life travesties? Are the people themselves living, breathing travesties, a mockery and a betrayal of the dignity of labour, the idea of community and class solidarity? Is the poem itself a travesty, a species of half-truth, a compromise, a lyric lie? Is it all of the above? Or neither? "Travesty" in its modern usage carries several connotations: it evokes something that fails in its representation of the values and qualities it purports to portray. In this sense the poem is a travesty, all art is, as language can only ever be a compromise with lived experience, our own or anybody else's. The poem acknowledges this. "Travesty" also denotes something that fails to do what it is intended or expected to do. In this sense, the poem is again a travesty, in that it is art that offers neither solace nor enlightenment. There is no punchline and no moral; the text, like the poverty it describes, is circular and cyclical, unending, repetitious.

And yet, what is also unintended and unexpected is the drama, richness and occasional flourish of beauty that rise up from the South London ring roads and fried chicken shops. And "travesty" here has a positive, radical meaning: a kind of defiance in the face of all you're told you are, and everything your life amounts to; everything we are supposed to mean or be. "Travesty" carries within itself notions of distortion and disguise; of burlesque, grotesque and parody. And so this sequence confronts working-class existence, my working-class existence with these tools. There's humour here, at least I intend for there to be humour here. In this place, in moments of extremis, even madness might be mobilised to wrestle and withstand a reality that assaults us as overwhelming and overwhelmingly ugly. There's a very different poem I could have written, "accentuating the positive", valorising working-class life and existence. A tender poem, perhaps, looking with love at what's good and decent here. Sure. It's been said before now that my poems focus almost obsessively on all that is harsh, unpleasant and unredeemed. But that's my life, these are my feelings; this is what I see and hear and smell, and whatever I have that is decent or good or tender is bound about and buried beneath all that is less lovely, that grates and jars and menaces and generally sticks in the throat. It's easy to be tender and loving to a beautiful child, no?

I still believe that if you don't see the swagger, the élan, the humour and the loveliness in the place or in my words, then that's your myopia speaking and not mine. There are other poems that sing about affinity, not alienation; but alienation has its own poetry, and that deserves expression too. What to say and how to sing when we have no sense of ourselves, when we feel lost to both to our present communities and our personal histories? When we feel defeated or deafened by politics, when we find no solace in faith, and when material existence grinds us down a little each day. This is the music I've made from that feeling, and to make that music, to create a space to say these things in a system and society that's trying to shut your stories down, to sand the edges off, to render your experiences and insights "acceptable" for mass consumption, then this is also a radical act. Not the most important act, not the biggest, but a beginning. This was my beginning. Show me yours.

///
Raptures & Captures
Poems by Fran Lock

"Keep your mind in Hell and despair not."

—Saint Silouan

"Pessimism of the intellect, optimism of the will."

—Antonio Gramsci

Contents
Raptures & Captures

Updated Introduction...*i*

In need of saints...103

Justina (Saint Justina)...105

Sebastian in Soho (Saint Sebastian)..106

Uncumber / Wilgefortis speaks..107

Bury the wren (Saint Stephen)...108

The girl with kaleidoscope eyes (Saint Lucy).........................110

Radical Savant, Newbury 1994 (Saint Francis).......................111

Our Aggie (Saint Agnes)...113

All the errors and mistakes (Saint Valentine)........................115

Rita of the White Bees (Saint Rita)...116

Saint Martin in Euston (Saint Martin of Torres)...................118

And Margaret is swallowed by Satan in the shape of a dragon (Saint Margaret)..120

Homobonus in Primark (Saint Homobonus).........................123

Enter Judith (Jael, Deborah) ('Saint' Judith).........................125

Anthony After All (Saint Anthony)...127

Rollox and his dog (Saint Roch)..128

Bernie (Saint Bernadette)...129

Imbolc (Saint Brigid)..130

Lamplighters..131

+

Prayers and Maledictions..135

Notes on the Poems..143

Note on the author..157

An updated introduction

By *Fran Lock*

'Keep your mind in Hell and despair not.' It's a stern injunction. It is also a radical one. Saint Silouan, we're told, struggled against demons. Specifically, he struggled against the demon of despair, against a feeling of abandonment, an absence of God's Grace. And so God spoke to Saint Silouan, gave him this electrifying ascetical credo, this moral imperative toward humility and hope. Just think about that for a minute. Not the genesis of the idea, but the idea itself. It's Gramsci's exhortation too, his riff on Romain Rolland: 'pessimism of the intellect, optimism of the will', which requires of us more than a cleareyed acknowledgement of how bad things are, but an understanding that the conditions for revolutionary change do not yet exist. It's asking us to live in the world as it is, not as we would have it; sustaining a mood of vulnerable and sceptical questioning, even when the truth is bruising. It means a stalwart refusal to abdicate responsibility; to acknowledge our own implicatedness in all that besets us. It means not isolating ourselves in the self-protective echochambers of social media. It means seeing the worst and believing in better.

For Gramsci, change could only be brought about through organised, disciplined action. Specifically, through the vanguard party seeking to establish aworkers' state. Gramsci's optimism—his hope—is a verb, not a noun. This hope exists—can only exist—in its active expression. In which case, whether or not we feel hope is irrelevant, what is important is trying to imagine ways of being hopeful.

As I said, a stern injunction. It's an injunction I *still* wrestle with every day. Mental illness is a fucker. It doesn't offer much by way of escape or sustenance. There are days I feel abandoned too, an abject absence of hope or love. Under such conditions it's hard to preserve faith, political or personal. I look at the world sometimes, and I find it almost impossible to reconcile with or accept. People are cruel, complacent, bigoted; the planet is perishing, culture is eroding. I withdraw into myself, afloat in the black amniotic of depression. I forget who I am, my responsibilities, my affinities, to the people and things I believe in and love. And I can't do one single sodding thing about those feelings. It's the way I'm wired, the vexed result of everything that makes a life. I can't change how I feel, but I don't have to accept those feelings as absolute reality. I can remind myself I am not my worst day. I can know, even if I can't perceive it, that goodness exists. That there are things worth fighting for, moments of perseverance, triumph, joy.

I cannot do that alone. Nobody can. And that's the thought this book emerged from. This isn't a religious book. It's not properly a Christian book, or even a Christian-Communist one, although that's the soil its roots are firmly planted in. It's about the need within all of us for communities, stories, solidarities; for something greater than ourselves. This book isn't asking you to *believe* in the saints as figures with magical properties or powers, that's not what's being presented here. The figures in these poems are all struggling, in one way or another, with demons. They need a portion of transformative magic in order to survive.

The strength I draw from the lives and examples of saints is cumulative. They are links in a chain, part of a process so glacial as to be imperceptible within the span of an individual life; a process built on the steady, incremental gains of those who went before. The saints allow me to see myself as, in my own small way, a minor contributor toward momentous coming change. I hold onto this. While "resolution", "escape", "success", or any other form of personal satisfaction might not be forthcoming; while gratification is both imminent and deferred, this is not to say that my life has no meaning, that any individual life must be subordinated to the dictates of collective survival. Rather, the single self is suffused with and strengthened by a long chain of historical connection. While it is incredibly hard to reconcile crushing personal disappointment with this deeper, more profound socialist *hope*, that's precisely what we—as socialists—are called upon to do.

Some of these poems are exhortations and prayers; others subject the lives of saints to the distortional stresses of modernity. In many of the pieces the speaker embodies both the legend of the saint, and the desperate, urgent needs of those who fall under their patronage. This is deliberate. The saints are compelling *precisely* because they are people, human beings with the same frailties and failings as any of us. And yet they are people whose radical example, whose deeds and teachings, rise above those failings to accomplish marvels. Tory Britain in the last decade has been a terrible place and time to be poor. More than ever we've needed those examples, those marvels. And more than ever we have needed to remember we are capable of them.

'Keep your mind in Hell and despair not'. The speakers in these poems rise from or confront their several Hells, which are also our own. They do so, I hope, with an equal mixture of anger and compassion, sensitised, always, to the human cost of our morally compromised pleasures, our conveniences, our "progress". Saint Homobonus is openly weeping in Primark, tearing fabric into strips with his bare hands, less in protest than in sheer incredulity at the degree of moral disconnect required to accept a world in which a factory worker's life is considered a fair swap for a shitty two quid t-shirt. Saint Sebastian follows with sadness and infinite sympathy a teenage rent-boy in Soho, a figure whose swaggering sense of agency has masked the exploitation he is subject to. The saints appear at all our scenes of selective deafness, willed, inertia, ethical amnesia; anywhere that people choose the path of least resistance. They appear to retune our attention toward the suffering of others, and they appear so that we who suffer know that we do not do so alone.

There's a good ol' lefty commonplace about prayer: that it's a way of absolving yourself of responsibility without actually having to do anything. It's an argument, I guess. But the prayers these poems incarnate are not prayers as daydreams or vague best-wishes, they're prayers as places of testimony, they're prayers as angry witnessing to pain, prayers as rallying calls and clarion cries. They are sites and occasions for protest. In prayer we coalesce around the common struggle. We listen and are listened to. We remember each other.

More than anything else, I see the speakers in these poems not merely as speakers, but as listeners. They understand that people deserve and are capable of better; that there is great courage, love and kindness in the most unlikely of us. The poems want to offer this space of solidarity. A communion. A communism.

In need of Saints

listen: on the furthest edge of my magical thinking somebody says
to suffer without love is a waste of pain. but who loves us? on days
when the eye of the world is a furnace of forgetting; we slide from
nowhere into *nothing* unremarked, but *marked*. times there's no
one else to share a slanted fate. our skies of disobedient blue. our
entropy, assessment, debt. on days when god is routine unrelenting
splendour; too fine and far a thing for comfort. cold light pressing
into temples. *who* is there for all the times we're surly, nervous
and compelled, down corridors and alleyways, and any place
a strip-light flickers, anywhere a slack luck lingers, fails? months
of malady and panic; asterism, augury, illiterature of omens, stones
and stars. long days sucking diesel fumes in freezing fog. to shoulder
the city's indifferent lore. a pain like tearing paper. pain like biting
through a glass. our spasms, cramps, and anticlimax, feverish
collateral. a lover's scorns and pauses, practiced pressure of a hand.
for tall hurts reaching up like trees to block the light. for days
that pale to finite shine in ugly towns of bleak taboo beside the sea.
for terrible things. this secret snow inside the globe of *self.*
for everything the present season spites or lacks, has no way back
from. listen: who will love us? when god's a bright bestriding
that we cannot know to name. us girls who can't believe. conform.
deform. do uneventful flesh. girls, with the lock-jaw logic of tetanus,
dread for days. and fearing death by water, men. girls are afraid
to say, afraid to name, afraid *of* speech. girls who kneel and creep but
cannot pray. where emptiness is ultimatum. girls defer to a four-letter
word, to the *force majeure* of shame. the mind in spirals, bound
and prone. imagination, whinnying and insect, spits. the last nerve
fledging into flame. girls untongue a curse. in silence. with silence.
anything withheld. not *held,* but *handled* raw. and god is an unbodied
brilliance loose in the room, too shining-wide a thing for comfort.
everywhere, like gossip, moths. to be lost, at a loss, when crisis comes,
like now. and christ, as pure as a blank cheque, as hospital soap,
the standard hush of libraries. he cannot share recession's stink,

insomnia, this bare and complex dark without design. the mind
 unsteadied. how skin is ghettoed, got, is jettisoned or weathering in
bruising schools. or trapped in airless rooms on truant afternoons,
a twisted mess of pleats and seams. god *is good*, but god's too good,
and god aghast is faberge and satellite—is beaming his gold nonplus
in tempered waves. listen: *chavo*, what *is* prayer? in the ear or in
the air? the line between a *wish*, a *doubt*, the intelligent shape of noise.
what *is* prayer? a hope you hold becalmed in the bowl of your own
hearing. insensible shell, the ear that makes an ache of all our straining
after sound. to receive. to *be* received, just once. our narrowcasting
pulled from abject static, joyless aural dystrophy. sleight of word.
unheard, halfheard, unsaid. to be *received*. to turn. to turn into. tune
and turn to. women like ourselves, but strong. if saints are better
engines. *communion, union, union...* system of our own sleek coping.
they're coming through. they're gilding mildewed bedrooms. tiered
light in their tangled hair. tears. as tangible as cats. a fleeting shape
that swells if spoken to.

Justina

"The agonising pincer-jaws of Heaven" —Patrick Kavanagh

demure, in some uremic light, slight and tawny-
joyless girl, who ached to slip her border town
of asters, grasses, galingales, of chronicle and gossip.
longed for barefoot forest paths, for holm oak
and flambeau, a peace the golden silence drives
in particles and waves. her days are spent among
the catechists and lackeys; masochists, philanderers,
their maxims and their tactics. justina sits and spins –
with pitchfork spinsters, women spitting pins
and sucking thread. she dreads the stooping creed
they court; each braided mane, ybounden breath.
a cheap intrigue, the axis of this dark default. the way
they corset thought, compress her flesh, deforming
fleetness into limp and simper: each peach slipper's
satin pinch. her cinched waist. spancelled, laced.
a hedging step. her laundered form, a crease they
curb with heat, a pleat they iron into air. her long
hair held like reigns. she dreams of surefoot
mountain paths; to spring these shantung snares.
a resin scent released where e'er she steps, free to
sigh among the pines, or else incline to sleep.
and in that dim clairvoyant sprawl, justina runs
with unicorns, her anxious palomino shape is
twisting through the trees. to shrug her skin,
to spite the lathe and lanyard of desire. monopolists,
apologists, the tired ideas they aim like arrows.
to sprint and flyte with hart and sparrow; vault
the lichened convent walls, to juke between
the teeming hives, to call their golden sanctums
home. copse be her sorority. these honey-sweating
combs, her own.

Sebastian in Soho

and the night sends your thoughts through their imbecile
circussing, yellow and red. through goblin markets, gardens
and squares, global economies, pockets you plunder for loose
change. *spare any change?* a fine rain weaves this scene
from silver thread. the way your form is wreathed in smoke,
the way your memory's acid-etched, both delicate and stricken.
you smile, old men are smitten, knit caresses into cudgel, musk,
and muscle; the lisp and skirmish of desire. their numb tongues,
your button fly, the wire inside tuned tight. the night sends thought
on headless errand. wrecked in step, befriend the blind, insensate
dark of squats and stairwells, booths in basement bars, parked cars,
attics leaking fractured light. where old men thrill to your fickle
swagger. agate-eyed, a creature of preternatural pearl. young, so
young and supple with hunger. there's a silver bell inside
of you, it rings its singing summons in the gut; bends you double,
sends each cornered thought careering. a silvered hell inside of you.
seven dials, st giles, where compass points cross purposes. fret at
intersections, sweat and tethered, guided by a bad idea. by *minor
indiscretions*. you're a kite caught between fist and firmament.
hard cash incubating in an open palm. these are the *good ol' days*,
where doorways gape with plague, with trade. soho plies her
somnolent commerce, pushing her luck. lean boys suction-cup
each stuttering kiss. and you, you are as *full of arrows as an urchin*,
want silver spoons to stir your nakedness to nectar. too many
irons in the fire. greek street breeds this bitter-dark polari; parlay
of wounds, and wands, of old men indulging their emptiness
in denim and indifference. and you, you are *adulterated*
by arrows, dulled and torn. thread-bare, firstborn, still standing—
just. bearing up the bed you're bound to, eyes rolled skyward,
stoic ghost.

Uncumber / Wilgefortis speaks

(for J.E)

grant me a buccaneer look, dear god, something akin
to my ferrous will. i'll schlep my bulk in army boots.
let grown men doubt, i'm woman still. i *hope* i make
him puke, unstomach his lunch in his lap. i'm *thrilled*
he's drunk on queasy pique. i'm tidal-wide and tired
of his crap. to perform their pasteurised beauty, god,
is a travesty of native grace. mine will not be the earth
they scorch. i will not bleach or scourge my face. grant
me this brackish coppice of leaves; these wiry mongrel
coils of fleece. i shall bestride his blank unease. he'll
boil and gnash than give me peace. his fists will boast
a commotion of stones, he'll spit illiterate disgust. but
better subject to his hate, than quailing object of his lust.
grant me a buccaneer look, dear god. not some unsexed
funnel of moulded flesh. a brightly banderol mane,
dear god, and wit and freedom while i've breath.

Bury the wren

(For M.M-H)

there's a line of wet black birds on the edge
of the roof like a string of blown bulbs. one
old crow with a wing out crooked as a pirate
flag. silence. caches under concrete slabs.
fly-tipped sofas sag. gulls pull bags from bins.
off-white-outgrown christening gowns. women
with striated faces puff and shove at buggies
full of shopping. dogs on their paranoid errands,
feinting at fences. game-show snarl on rotties,
staffies, pits. and there's these kids, who shit
where they live: ringtone cynics in ski-masks
carrying pool cues. baseball bats. and lately –
knives. scrape a screaming grace from treads
of trainers, tyres; black grout between the tiles.
little town of conquest and vomit. 'ead the balls
counting your *weregild*, smirking. here, your smile
betrays you. young men hunt in packs. doped,
provoked, with nothing in between. unprincipled
insomnia. the nights they tigered. tyranny.
defective weather-system, orange, blue. on
days like these i think of you: toking, broken.
the chipboard walls you're yoked to. and cars
on bricks all stripped for parts like medieval
catafalques. landfills, fields and edgelands.
acne, aggrogasm, scar, the hieroglyphs
of harm. i think of you. st stephen's day,
we pray for strength in times of persecution.
but did you *cast forth sparks?* make perfect
love a lightbulb moment. no. all blood, no lust.
we pray to forgive. i walk the river where you
lived. stretched like black magnetic tape. my

body could break this depthless plane, intent
as a spade. pray to forgive. the sides
of your head, spoiling for stones. nickel
blade that nicked the bone. these stupid
streets like arteries. the rocks they threw.
the hate they give.

The girl with kaleidoscope eyes

'tis the year's midnight, old women work, convening fevered
dooms for child brides. ourselves included. i want none, won't
come to my wedding bed, unblinking and bedazzled as a lamped
rabbit, nor chew on the roots of boreal tansy for pain. some girls
get themselves ossified on mogadon, some swept up in a dreamy
chaos of watered silk and catalogue furniture; seed pearls,
bouquets, baby names. don't blame those girls. i'm not those girls.
don't see myself interred in a new-build cul-de-sac skinny from
pills. i've seen those girls, pot-bound in caterpillar boots, combing
their scaldy ponytails until their scalps come red. i won't go to
my wedding bed. my dreams are carmelite-fantastic, agnes in
a mantilla of stars, and mary's velveteen pin-cushion heart. *'tis
the year's midnight*, old women work, for patrimony, promissory
notes. sisters scheming meagre looks to skeins of carrick lace.
fortunes fold in their taffeta laps. corsage, cortege, a cake the size
of a child's coffin, all in white. an off-pink smile they pipe like icing.
once, and only once. then life's all unguents, ichors, gruels and soups.
i give my dowry away. my dreams are the reckoning splendour
of god, of a father with arteries larded with love. not men with
their capital passions, swinging their poesies like clubs. oh, saint
lucy, in the sequinned magisterium of your great gurlesque regard,
come save me. you were like us, betrothed, denounced by feudal
louses, solemnising lust with vows. speak up for us girls condemned
to the unmiraculous lights of council houses; to melancholy and telly
novella, pillowslips, slipknots, the daily face-ache. lucy, they tried to
defile you, to make you a plough, or a faggot, or any inanimate thing.
you would not budge, you would not burn. the eyes they prized
and held in tongs: eccentrically facetted, carat and glass. *'tis the year's
midnight*, and mine. i need your second sight. tight new buds, their
wakeful flourish. see my way clear towards the light.

Radical Savant, Newbury 1994

illiteratus. our extrovert. you're up on high. the would-be
bypass hums to your inner condition: the rackety anthems
of various birds, their whoop and glut. you're good at that;
the folklore of each folded leaf: wild mushrooms, clustered
buds, the cud of their classless names. every bended stem.
oh, you are not afraid of fires or spiders, dysentery, the crack
of a fallible branch,or *any*thing. my fitful dreams are full
of falling, clawing the caving ceiling from my open mouth.
not you. you love the giddy risk of wet turned earth and vertigo.
you meet each morning where it lives: a-twist in the ice
of upper air.

all you boys poured out of border towns, aggrieved
and ungrammatical, unkempt; your hair the ragged
pennants of a losing war. your doctrine is ecology
and unwashed consequence. on the tv you're known
as bony wrist in shapeless sleeve; known by the grim
set of your jaw. but *you* are different: even when
the forecast is a cord of wood and concrete poured on open
fields, you never rage or bait or brawl. you will not fight,
you do not yield. you make a keen compulsive peace
your sword, your shield, a light you hold in front of you.

we called you *hippie, dilettante, trust-fund-crusty* too afraid
of metaphoric *dirt* to brace his faith against the brick, the bat,
the boot. but we are wrong. and you are not *as passive as
a mattress,* but anchored in the aching soil, a thickened root.
and you will not be moved. *zealot*—maybe—who looks on
life, is stung to love. for *every*thing, for *every*one. you told
me once that what you want *is man complete, and better than
his bad ideas.* by which is meant grim cities and the misweaved
mess of money. now of all our lost or gone, yours are the words
i still recall.

illiteratus, first among maverick cavalries, feeding
a fox from your hand in the freezing fog. or the way
you charmed the shepherd dogs away from their angry
handlers. i see you still, dancing like a filament
of rancid wool before the fire, before you pitch and sway
and fall. the way you raved and made your *entire body
tongue*. the tumble of your tangled joy. the way you
seemed so young—

at other times so sad. i see through smoke the fragments
of your antic form, delirious against the dawn. mine were
eviction's pin-wheeled fists. yours the lone, forlorn, unarmed—
defenceless and defending. in the strange momentum
of collapse, the whorl snails smashing underfoot. your halo's
framed by coloured flags, your vegan cheekbones smudged by soot.

Our Aggie

and it wa'nt the way you say. not some
spacey cherub in a fresco. it wor aggie,
insufficient-shaped in too-big padded
jacket, blue. an' fire wor blue. roman
sort poured petrol, intensified its eating.
dopey fucker, flames don't part like pages.
flames is wrapped all round her juss'
like clingfilm on a new tattoo. pressing,
pressing, pressing, til' fire's the only
thing tha's holding her together. angry
men, when, up behind the jagged sheets
of prefab tin, she didn't find 'em funny.
aggie let the young 'un go. *fly away
home*. didn't like that. well. s'all
the same: suitors, state, men wiv big
omnipotent fists, meting out
the earworm of their secret: *you tell
a soul, we'll fuck you up*. tell a soul.
angel on an xmas tree. guadalupe
on a dashboard, smelling of chemicals.
angry man, scrabbled her smile to
one broke catastrophic curve. *drag*
or *drug* her by the roots of her
hair, glittered and sprawled in 'is
playroom. but aggie kept smiling
a private smile to god. kept some
inner thing alive: tricky candle
he couldn't blow out. didn't like
that. well. he socked her, stamped.
like a cowboy with bullets under
his boots. knocked her cold. put her
on the fire. vague stream of
ghostly photons. but it wor aggie

still. even after the knife. pried
and parted. scarred. still. some fluke
of grace soul-shininess, irrevocable,
rose.

All the errors and mistakes

times this town's a wet knot swoll inside of me.
unpicked along its edges, frayed but fast. i fast.
i cannot eat. speak and the whole world leaks in
through my mouth. or think. except on god. how
form is thrashed to foam; is wracked or channelled.
man is made of tides. times i long to spill the rich
weather of my sickness. tremors, tumours, any
way the bloodshot eye is hounded, barks. coloured
blubs are blowing all along the promenade. my shark-
infested circuitry. i am the sea i sink in. time. it's all
my story. things you think you know: this sharp
intake. the bitten tongue. the strap, the spoon. to
pin my flailing meat to floors. or else what legend
pretties: intentions and betrothals. spotlit, singled
out. how chaucer said *whan euery bryd comyth
there to chese his make.* mistake. love unspun me.
threshed in sweat. am spurned, am torn. to sulk,
convulse. adrift, bereft. my skewed surmise,
incurable. or no. under the emperor, under the axe,
the madness of crowds. most lacerable skin of me.
might have saved a girl with eyes in crisis. pressed,
like doctored marbles to the light until
they rediscovered blue. i can't recall. i fell in fast,
i lived in fear. the pressure builds. am copious
and crazed with flowers. a phone box, grim
confessional. times the gaunt stunt of my body
is much too much. the final blindness men call
god. occulted i, or clarified. writhing isn't ecstasy.
chocolate stains on satin pillows. to be myself.
delete. make new.

Rita of the White Bees

pray for us, for the girls like green splinters, their pierced
reveal unfolding in small towns running on skeleton crews;
for the pageant-hearted girls who burst like bright ideas into
backseats, bikinis, the blessable dream of being human; for
the too skinny stay-awake girls, living on rice wine and red
light, whose home is the typical *elsewhere* of exiles; for the
lip-glossed gonzo girls, those high femme fatalists, all cried
out; for the lost girls, giddy and groped on, coked to their
stoic ponytails, shiny and slick and swinging like whips; for
the headlong girls, barefoot and bracing themselves in a bus
lane, smiles like Saint Laurent scarves on fire, manic
and vampire; for the girls who went waning in wraparound
glasses to clinics and vigils; for the pub-crawled girls in
packs, in parks and lanes, alive with the loitering joy
of foxes; for the girls who fuck like stray cats come to
sad anatomical terms in the spongy summer nights of cities;
for the girls in ravenous warp speed, spinning, spun, till tears
collect in their cartwheeled eyes like sparks; pray for us, for
wasted girls with workshy serotonin, whose trestle cheekbones
grind on air; for the peep-toed girls with broken heels
and fake eyelashes, trafficking tears at a photo shoot; for
the lookbook, look back angry girls, whose *bad day* is
a black dress that goes with everything; for the bitch fight
girls, their raw collided atmospheres on fire, all cellulite,
venom, and celebrity perfume; for the girls whose hairdos
are stairways to heaven, whose pigments shiver in vintage
frocks, whose song is a storm in a borderline thought, who
tend their fetishes like flowers; for the girls, most of all,
who are their own witching hour, their jaundiced drama
dragging them down in the bump and grind of a tightening
gyre; for the girls whose vertigo is *not* the fear of falling, but
the fear of jumping; who are so entirely sick of this mingy,
yelping ethic men call *love*; for the girls who are no longer

young, whose unmade faces are empty airports; whose
bodies are the quarrels they are having with themselves;
for these girls, their madness lasting them out like a sensible
pair of leather boots. Patroness of Impossible Causes,
pray for us, that we might flip a decade's deadweight
like a mattress; gather our godspeed, walk away from
ourselves.

Saint Martin in Euston

miserere. monday is a man reduced to his bare
incident, a stain the pavement eats. a sharded
light is stalled between the concrete benches,
busses, cranes. drills compete, declare a complex
discord. everywhere the air is rutted, hurts.
and yet the earth turns still. the concourse fills
with factions, mobs, gym memberships, majorities
and miniskirts. miskiltered mouths. here are
the men who bury their piqued slang in mobile
phones, little kids who kick at pigeons; prêt
a manger sandwiches, the salaries and symptoms.
miserere. where kinship skitters, alleys end
in piss. this circus of averted eyes and shifted
weight. we wait in line for *black americano*.
cargo of feeble guilts. appropriate frown, a face
made plasticine with pity. melt. and *it is terrible*.
drink up, get out, and go, cocking deaf in
headphones, march like regiments or inmates.
off to work. high-ho!
            but then—
monday is a man, and when he speaks
the old *home* hails me; love becomes a wet
umbrella, sprung indoors. i felt—i saw—
i thought about saint martin, cutting his cloak
in two. *miserere*. it's *all too much*, sometimes.
the grim unfolded fact of it. the shit. how lips
are franked by sanction, shrinking into slur
and stoop and scuff. undifferent dirt. these
grounded birds. these ragged nails and filthy
cuffs. i saw—i heard—and in my head saint
martin stands, as naked as a maypole. his halo
weak and radiant-hard. the struggling fluorescence
of a lightbulb in a bedsit. backstreet, bus stop,

tarmac yard, this his kingdom. tears his shirt, his
hair, his skin to remnant whispers. but still,
there's not enough of him. can't cover
such a vast and shuffling need. *miserere*.
how love is this machine for stretching,
reaching, wretched, incomplete. here we
are in incomes, indecision, rolling our
eyes like pellets of bread in order not
to see.
                    but see!
saint martin through a megaphone, ranting
and antagonised: *what's wrong with you?
what's wrong with you?* and then you see.
and you cut your coat in two.

And Margaret is swallowed by Satan in the shape of a dragon

a dragon is a maggot in drag, mate. crunching
his numbers for status or grace, on afternoons
of pox and hoax; of pillories and guillotines. he
says *you're fit*. aggro, limbo, irrational sanction.
spittle and grist. and his slit-mouth is a letterbox
leaking shit. when a job is a coffin in drag, mate.
and the salaried factions laugh, insist. we're
itemised and spited, smote. and ghosts with
smokers' coughs are tearing paper into strips.
the disbelievers blink. a fungal light you wipe
from eyes. our poltergeists and skelly-bones.
boys with antisocial ankles, kicking off again.
i can't. i won't. *you will*, he says. this land
of wastes and graves; this land of face-ache
and malaise, of grating days and granite
stupor. *here, sign here, stand here, and sit.
lift your arms and walk unaided*, shift your
weight and wait your turn. *who said that
you've a right?* i know. i might have known.
a right to freeze, a right to burn. sentenced
and assessed. i tried. to rise. to stammer out
my mitigating pidgin. i am tried. and not all
fire is cleansing, clean. the mind is strewn,
astray. we hate him for his postures and his
logics. a tradition and a discipline, this hate.
it binds our sad *kumpania*. blind leads blind
leads blind. in circles. pervert a repetitive pain
in my cells to nothing you would grieve for.
box he ticks. i am not *sick*. i'm tired. insomnia
and sophistry, his principal munitions. i am
tied, and grafted to the bad idea he traffics in.
or stunted. culled. stunned by his scattergun
judgments. *what should i do?* a form to fill.

index of undesire. what's empty, spent. take
a number. take a seat. repeat. come back
tomorrow, abject and prompt at two. he's
sharpening his pencils like a homicidal
diplomat. the monitor, a flat blank stare
that pares you back to guilt and sinew. if
a maggot is a dragon in disguise, discuss.
this heat-sealed smile, this parody of nurse,
all instruments and principles and lipstick on
her teeth. *you're fit*, she says. for what?
a juiceless fuck to pay the rent? shelf-
picking, stacking-stock. the big, bad brassic
wreck of the week? for cringe and scrimp
and licking stamps. living off lint in the freeze-
dried dark, and a limescale soup i got from
the sally. to be eaten. by degrees. to be
consumed. to be aphasic, razored. scythed
and mauled beneath multiple glass moons.
averted eyes. the smell of bleach. these
clamant, saturated streets, their tightrope
variations. type. and pique. and wheeze.
his single infected design. he's putting
the squeeze on. we stilt-walk to suicide in
second-hand heels. a man whose head is
a worried knot. arterial tease from the non-
event girl. *for attention*, they said. to be free.
of hope. the pratfall of ideals. oh god,
to be calibrated incorrect. when the letter
makes landfall: *failed.* the profanity
of *benefit.* diagnosed, accused. to be refused.
refuse. rubbished and maimed at a formica
table. tenterhooks, imperatives, the way
they get you: snared and nailed to
the summit of disgust. a dragon is a maggot
on the sly. a machine that teethes and shits,

shits what it eats, that paves the streets
with vagrancy. with human shuck. we're
all the same. convicts and veterans, conscripts,
illegals. his spiracles gape. inmates and victims,
soilent green. he lives off this. off us. constipation.
sloth. to be *devoured*. by mute degrees. monster
of probability. a faecal greed. attrition we are
quarry of. debt moves in spirals like sharks.
spiders. earworm weaving threat from air. *you
do not deserve*, that double-edged sword. *sit
down. stand up. hold the back of the chair.*
the bony farce that death delivers. crescendo
of expendable flesh. all the savaged eye
contains. seen too much. can't feel my legs.
      can't catch - - - my breath.

Homobonus in Primark

where will it end? the long-sleeve t-shirts
sleep, all folded over themselves like bats.
black lycra's pirate sinew stretched to slack.
and tubes of ruined wool relax and lose
their shape. sleeves wear the gape of empty
snakes. disfigured fabrics frayed in heaps.
a woman shaking out the prissy ghosts
of a summer blouses, snagged on a hanger's
embittered caress. for *two pound ten!* each
pleat a gauntlet of skirmished thread, rough to
the touch. *it costs so little!* the woman said.
impossible pasture of rags, dear god! it costs
so very much. where will it end? i stroke
the mesh, the weft, the weave, from cheviot to
chiffon-cling. grope a glut of sturdy twills.
my hands surge out across an odyssey
of cotton, serge. and batiste gowns are
grown in rows like off-white heads of
lettuce. crisp and sleek. and underfoot,
the scattered wits of covered buttons. *look!
it's in the sale!* adrenaline and penny pinch.
cash canters horselessly between the heels.
hemlines. oh, i have loved the crushes
and the calicos, the way a seam will meet
like steadfast hands in payer. i have loved
the self-important bombazines and obsolete
brocades, stood in satin-transfix running
a bolt of blue charmeuse through my hands
like a live fish. but no, not like this. not
this way. the woman who sewed this dress,
her lungs are dressed in dust, disease.
her shoulders cramped askew. not like this,
a child in a stocking of sweat with eyes

as dull and flat as coins, his name a smudge
on a hot-wash label. the day that factory
became a dirt red funnel for human
grief. *it's just so cheap, dirt cheap!*
your cambrics, buckrams heresies.
and what's it worth, a life?
assiduous stitches, tucked and running.
in lame. gold is interwoven—secret
vein through common cloth. as pain
pursues its jagged course, in every
shirt you smooth and touch. i'll tear
these strips. they cost so much.

Enter Judith (Jael, Deborah)

a small town, ours, prolific in injury. dominion,
conspiracy, *fait accompli* down the local disco.
please walk with care. there's men round here,
chewing us names like wodges of flavourless gum.
down country lanes, a supernatural light declines
in lay-bys, slides off lockets, flannel laps; the red
bare shoulders seatbelts bite. where *girl* is
a ticklish purse of skin, trapped in the pouty depths
of a mirror, syncing her cherry-ripe lips to gloss.
where *girl* is a pageant of plastic barrettes; her hair
in platinum contrails, combing 'cross the cutty
dusk. in our town girls are everywhere, their bony
commonplace in braces, shorts. in terraced houses,
spilling out of cul-de-sacs, homogenised
and obvious; turned into pillars of table salt on
corners outside our price. their hips and rigmarole,
bop and shrug and panda pop. please walk with
care. where men are buttoned into their absolute
names. this one, a coronary with personal plates,
and a hand on the small of a narrow back, kinked
like the clasp of her cheap brooch. this one in boots
and promises and gab. this one in wheedling reproach.
or a weary cool girls gravitate towards. another is
sweets and a warm interior out of the rain on the long
way home. it's a tiny town, the width of a cell. us girls
have made escape our one fixed star. contortionists
and inmates, girls. please walk with care. an open door,
a graspy brittle light within. a future you could make
a fist around has made a fist around us all. enter
judith. judy. moi. in plimsolls, gingham, scimitar.
through the car park up the youthy, eyes front.
an immaculate braid like a velvet rope, blue-black.
my implausibly pink-white mouth is plumping

meagre vowel to sound. i pay my pound and wait,
watch simultaneous monkeys bumping foreheads
on the floor. i don't wait long. he steers me between
gravy-smelling curtains, down a corridor lit
by nicotine stains on the ceiling, his own luminous
teeth. i keep my hand on the flap of my satchel.
inside is algebra and balisong, tampons and apples,
a highland dirk; is scramasax and gym slip,
a razorblade and a londis bag. in the back room
he butters and fumbles. wine in polystyrene
cups. i spit mine into the cushions. his i ginger
up with mammy's sleepers, watch his eyes
slide into bewitchment, writhe my skinny
pelvis to a popular song. he gasps, he reaches,
fails and drools. i grab my tools. a small town
ours. faces made asymmetric with shame. girls
without names, girls who become their own out-
of-focus photos, flail through life lost count of
and forgotten, walled up behind their silence
like medieval nuns. knife like a spring-loaded
butterfly. machete settles on his throat. an awl
to the side of the skull. to crash through
and *transfix his temples*, to sever his head
and wend back through the streetlamps
blinking on, like a little boy tired of more
innocent games. where the dirt washes off
and dinner awaits. yellow mash heaped
between two crocked plates.

Anthony After All

nothing is lost. luck merely leaves on a broomstick shrieking.
such is life. look, here's the fervent heart, and here's the missing
page. nothing is lost. but gone grotesque, on barbitone, ergotamine,
and fear applies its nitrate to a nerve. but don't lose heart. button
up against the world, its banging brassic chill; its nosey parkers,
bowler hats, and bus conductors. loveless. *all* froth and *no* coffee.
but still. well. i mean. and i would know, have tied another knot
in hurt's florid hanky, sat alone and smoked my lip to blister. but
hey, hang on, nothing's lost. the winning slip, the shilling for
the meter. this i know. even the evident wrecks at the seaman's
mission, their faces three-fold franked with categorical despair,
might suddenly come with a gust of *don't do it again, matilda!
oh, mister porter, what a silly girl i am!* and in unlit bedsitting
rooms you catch at spirit gleanings, crepuscular proofs of god
in the nodding dusk. even the old. lags and soaks, stirring
their porridge, concussed in an overcoat, slumped on a train,
anywhere a kiss unsticks itself from mouths. all that mob, or
heavies, schlepping the length of the country for a well-worn
cause. the lowly unenlightened, fleshpots, petite-bourgeoisie,
their snaggletooth empires built upon bones. anyone might find
it. music, strike these idle instruments to life. can't separate
the error from the comedy. now, there it is. isn't that better?
a laugh. a bell pealing on purpose. like a hyper-real lotus,
a split-screen smile.

Rollox and his dog

(For Cam, and Lil' Miss)

ma heid's mince, maimed for memory, shambling
intae the samey dark, an scunnered with the drudge
of it. come tae some flyleaf land and rest, ma dog
and me. an even here, the crackdaws rake their sharp,
selecting eyes across ma body while i sleep. but dog
will watch: centurion, ma starkest nurse. before
the dog some bawdy-head was always stomping me
tae shite, on nights ah pined and wagered in; learned
a lisping plenary through broken teeth. ah miss the sea,
a rife and restless inexact. ye can't go back. a special
pain with clockwork at its root. an sea's a grey
prevailing; when ah dream, its nagging vastness mithers
me. ye can't go back, an dog alone the lighthouse;
keeper of ma secrets. streets are hard, where every
unwashed mouth's a flag; where hipsters eating bijou
meat step over ye. get skelpit lugs and spit on, times.
an addict is an antique child, will break if shaken,
ragdolled out of doorways, kicked into the blink
and flicker of the wild blue nee-naw. dog, ma only
angel, come to terraform the soft tundra of the heart.
ah followed dog out the town, down the crow road,
up along the goat path—away, o'er bramble trap.
away, o'er whinhedge, nettlebed, moonwort in
the wreck of mortared walls, the gorse, the moss,
the furze and fern. the wood is full of invisible
listeners, but dog abides. we sleep in a blind dyke,
some crofter's hollow, under stars. an ah shiver, but
her eye looks without language, holds ma image
like a deep lake takes itae itself a sinking stone.
dog brings me meat, she lickit me. involuntary god
this whole long sickness we are riding out together.
one day ah will show her the sea. as sure as dog
taught me the line between *a creature* an a *beast*.

Bernie

our lady of lourdes in a laminated light, reflected
by the hardwood floor. a school where girls curated
braids; where girls had the fragrant names of saints,
a counterfeit feminine endlessly. and smiling eyes
like cruel lunettes. the bridgets and the bernadettes;
the katherines, scoured or salty. but only she was
bernie, as crass as *le cachot*, standing in the inelastic
socks of poverty; heavyset and trembling; *without
the wit to squeeze a spot*, they said. i disagree. bernie
saw the virgin: blue wheel spinning, soliciting sparks;
she ate the grass that grew in parks, knelt to drink
from stagnant streams. they said that she was *loony*.
i disagree. her dreams were imperious seizure, faith
as all-assailing brightness, light sent raving through
a prism. and why not? soubirous fetched wood
and went without, and only later learnt to read. i
believe in bernie's virgin, soaring force that lifts
you up above the body, school or self. girls there
didn't know, their faith was tattle and spasm, a reflex
in the fingers, a gossipy dysphoria that knew no
joy; that kept their saints like gimmicks in a gilded
box. soubirous was poor. and now the eager lips,
the rich kissers of wounds. and now the swag
and silky swagger of communion. now—ah, but
they can keep it. i'm with bernie, the grace of her
wotsitty breath, the seven pallid tallies on
her lineated wrists.

Imbolc (Saint Brigid)

inch out into the proving light, and carry
my *brídeóg*; crosses of reed, my gridle
of rushes, sunwise round the clootie well.
there is a spell, to turn the church to oak,
the stone to bread, the water into beer. i'm
no man's child, i know. i'm any name
you'd rip from wind, on rags. you'd wipe
up blood. goddess into abbess. this full
moon provokes the pagan pique in you.
either neither thing is true, or both. its both—
i hung my chaplet in the hawthorn, swore
i saw a vision. the tongue falters on the cusp
of honey. forgive my being born, i yearn
for sweetness, tasted graves, am sure to
end inelegant. biddy, help me. spectre
of the tresses. green hole in the ground,
this fork in the road, is conscience
enough for snow. i've calloused hands,
and scabs on my knees from kneeling. to
be as others are, fallible and fertile. to be
free. offal. awful. offering. to offer up,
this miserable legacy of rent meat. i'm no
man's child, i know. my father was a blazing
house, car on a fire, abandoned by a custom's
post. my father was the coaly night that lards
your limbs like soap. inch out into
the proving light, and consecrate myself
to rage; a large eye hanging in the branches.
a large eye blinking from the bottom
of a spring.

Lamplighters

how life is cold sometimes. sleepers of ice hold
open the jaws of the world. the way it is: consecrated
to the clock, encroached upon, impeded. limned in
the monitor's off-white fire. but somebody said that
we can be heroes. maybe all we can *be* is kind. our
splintered tribe: arriving, sudden and unlevel, born
forward of ourselves in time. temporal defectors. cut
through a living thicket of histories. set a bonfire in
a forest. oh, to *be heroes.* to forge, without precedent
or shelter. the strange, estranged, the stray. maybe all
we can do is good. to keep in mind we're linked in
light across the nervy breadth of each decade.
the fire we breathe, the flames we throw,
the fickleness of miracle. the razored strut of any
savvy magic. way it is: men becoming silhouettes
in windows, writhing stains against the double-
glaze. there is no *nine-to-five.* the slow, coronial
process of *work* capsizes us in corridors. the verdict
bursts—a bomb that knocks us squat, and all our
towers: *this is it.* yes. all we can be is kind. capital's
cruel manoeuvres. busy fingers work to untwist all
that is still human in us. long nights of grievance
and fatigue. to beat a word to pearl. to prize each
shining filament from sense, to press them into
pyrotechnic palsies, make something shining, good.
how life is cold sometimes. wrestling and effort.
when phrase becomes a mermaid's tail, improbable
and argent. how art must be the utmost of our reaching.
to signal back. across the steppe. defeatist slopes of inner
space. this too is prayer. to call our others forth: besotted,
filigreed, defiled, in all their schizoid soldiering. the most
we can *be* is kind. in narrow rooms where language
needs to crouch. an ugly talk that holds all autopsies in

common. to send the spirit tangent, plagued, to sing it
discomposed, to tell the eider stuff of midnight. lavish,
mercenary blue. to do this out of *hope*, the place where
wish is cindered into *ritual*. theirs are steadied kennings,
the ceremonials of stone. let ours be sudden rainbow's
rightness. love, elect of memory. the way we live: to practice
impossible whim. to hang our yellow lanterns crooked, from
the corner of each page.

Prayers and Maledictions

Prayers and Maledictions

i

Deliver my soul from the sword; my darling from the power of the dog
—Psalm 22:20

when we're dead what is left will belong
alone to the doggedly stupid. this i have
foreseen. dread, most subtle syndrome,
our tedious fever, most fascist emergency.
it is three a.m., and here in the badlands
we're trawling the shipwrecked network.
clickbait and twitterstorm. thin-skinned
insights, *social justice*. these *faces*, this
face. is a bland hoax youth parading long.
hot, wet summer; our dissident friends
have sewn themselves into their black
balaclavas. a failed state's spreading
like a fatal stain. monsoon season now,
the lunatic solar. fingertips flirt with
a *sinister failure* common to all. paralytic
light that dries republics out like spots.
molecular legions, uv rays. flesh, infernal
terraform. when we're dead. trump will
pick our corpses clean. utmost trump,
conspicuous *enfant*, in the tantrum of his
tyranny. *all* those drowsy profiteers.
sleepwalk us to ecogeddon, ecogasm.
eco. echo, echo. *oh lord, why have you
forsaken me?* and now the enemies are
arriving. homunculoid fuck-spawn, stung
into carbon; a palm oil posture. too
little too late. they tidied our psalms to
sum, to datastream. america's masochist

vowels are soft in their mouths. purveyors
of the pervert-real. reorganise the light
to waco. when we're dead. the viral griefs
we feed on. the black bloc posse strut. our
condemned men assert their smoke. tonight
the city flaunts its cold extortions. motorcade,
chinook. the sky is full. a leering wealth they
close a road for. grim umbilicus of bunting.
howling students, soaked by dirty rain. this
trump *is shit straining to shit.* through the eye
of a needle, down necks missing their heads.
money, his most grievous colonic, most tedious
fever, his fascist emergency. they are selling
off the hospitals, patients and all. they are
selling my body. principalities and latitudes,
territories with tribal names, older than
the sweat off satan's sack. they will pour
concrete and cord wood, and no one will
remember my parables or massacres.
the exile's body is a total geography. for
that wall of outraged mouths, the body's
a vacuous carnivore, a cushiony mascot,
its own padded cell. *oh lord, why have you
forsaken me?* greed is a fire through their
foam interiors: *take back control.* from
darkies and gyppos and jews. from a terror
of unpronounceable names. from the groping
nausea of pity. recitations, favours, chants,
a pulse they borrow from a baseline. i read
their manifesto. wheedling earworm, written
large on mesh-back caps. crowds are plausible
cacophony. are foreign policy as power ballad.
when we're dead. the victims, the resistors.
let those who come after go free. deliver
them, from sermons, sanctions, assault, insult.

from tory town's devious gothicking. on days
hope isn't a turtle dove, but a twenty-four
carat crowbar. let there be saboteurs, ninjas.
cross-fit bruce lee motherfuckers,
the glammy vegan brave. it is three a.m.
our matrix is an a-z of grim commercial lust.
deliver them, dear god, from grunting fact,
abuse of sex. the slow machine that wants
to grind their hollow bones to cochineal. new
breed. this razored helix spinning. mutinous
corkscrew, golden revolt. when we are dead
what is left will belong to the lickers
of broken windows. heads of state as lead
balloons. unless. or else. we reach. just
watch. this space. connect. repeat.

ii

Because the poor are despoiled, because the needy groan, I will now rise up
—Psalm 12:05

worm exults in utter wealth. harangues,
fatigues, redundancies. worm is the clown
prince of outsourcing; you will apply for
your old position at half the pay, and like it.
worm has spoken. a pessimist's rhapsody,
protected conversation. i am in love with
a man who wears this bleak disfigurement
in sigils. with syndicalists and scoundrels,
a host of delicate reprobates. worm has
a drooping, bloodless creed. worm is an
obscene gesture; is a raised middle finger
minus its fist. scion of garbage, the motley-
objectified. worm is both the creditor
and the currency. i am in love with a man
most of all, who funnels his fluent shape
through cotton shirts, a collar's stiff
complaint, the flaccid greed of office
wonks, and still remains himself, against
the worm. worm is a boneless hoop,
rolling through open-plan offices, is
doing hr for the vampire bourgeoisie,
is busy filing his *realistic* smile in
triplicate. we know him well. one green
thumb turned down toward our guilt:
*did you break a sweat today? did you
stop to eat? did you feel the sun on your
back?* worm is mounting his desk
like a pulpit, accounts become his
corporate elegy. i am in love with
a man who would skull-fuck the schedule's

seamless verboten! and i take his name
into the city against the worm. his name
is a cherry stalk, tied by the tongue.
to be agile with desire. to be alive,
among fences and detention centres,
sentry boxes, closed circuit televisions,
prisons, prisoners; the aberrant
and lacerated forms of interns,
competitors, criminals and victims.
worm exults in utter wealth. his,
a throbbing pirouette through
densest meat. our emperor of disgust,
our empire of disease. a black soot mien.
a rotten pulp. his, debt's queasy
gimmick, death and taxes. taxed.
to death. and i love a man who leaves
his shirts soaked and balled on
the floor, folded in on themselves
like impressionist roses. and i know
in our house with mould on the walls.
and i know on our straggling litter-
strewn streets. and i know on
the night's insomniac tightrope.
      love is a shield and spade
against worms.

iii

in the presence of enemies

I am thus not in front of judges, but in the presence of enemies; so it would be quite useless to defend myself. Also, I have no fear of any sentence that you may pass on me, while protesting nevertheless with energy against this substitution of violence for justice, for this frees me in the future of any inhibition against repaying the law with force.

—Louis-Auguste Blanqui, from his Defence Speech, 1832

hope springs ridiculous on instagram. all that *bitch, please*. all that piglet erudition. where hope is a cut-price paraphrase. oh, malevolent rent-a-quotes. you hordes, you stasi queens of shade. grief is the upper limit of your kitsch, your skin some luscious uniform. big fella was talking horseshit though a megaphone. *what is to become of us?* the odour-neutral future. yes, demilitarized sublime. to pick through our city. to live inside a city, disfigured into labyrinth, cradling our broken phones. oblivious eyes, cracked in parallel, their staggered blink and fold. so many screens. so many eyes. and to scavenge their blank expressions for warmth. no one can be this hungry and be wise. this feed is bottomless monarchy. money our deathly, trending tallow. money, suctions that corrupt as they console, the dark *there, there*, a fat mouth being bled. i saw him, an abscessed nerve, thin fang, milked transparent. money is his laxative. i saw him, he is spoofed pork. he is hope, sprung crouch in human shape. a school of fiscal eunuchs moon the ruins of a church. receptacle for cortisone and stale caffeine, my brain. it aches. the internet has spoken. sectarian and bestial, we will be stop-

and-searched and search-and-seized and rounded
up. indexed, sectioned. assimilated, scattered. her
eye is an umbrella, *angerlund*. to live inside her
largess like a pauper lunatic. her prying touch,
impersonal as porn. every day my glitching pulse,
my panic. my myotonic capsize. on the train to
work we're racks of swinging meat. and oh, you
row of whitened smiles, shock troops to her soft
policing. now, poet is an ugly velvet buzzword.
now, the *near-insane* symmetry of her face. she's
faking. fake, gilded fiend. jackal-headed goddess
of the new conviction. useless floating lobe. poetry
is straightened like a smile is stretched. oh,
wonderland. most serviceable crocodile. poetry.
these feeble anglo glossaries. is so much lawful
motherfucking. don't *bitch, please* me. all of us
connected by hot magnetic threads. politico,
that crucified mooncalf googling himself to
death. i've seen your world. your world is
vivisected beyond remedy. your world is
vivisected out of any recognition. someone
comes to repossess my sanctioned hemispheres.
much justice, such money: conjoined twins,
dressed in the lockjaw of identical violence.
who's sorry now? and what do you intend to do
about it? the world weathers its long vegetable
atrocity. all our broken exits. *angerlund*.
panopticon, monocle without an eye, hovering.
'merica. incessant and beseeching mouth.
inevitable, absolute, replete with teeth,
predatory and ritzy. 'merica. a million vanilla
skeletons, each limb a brooch secured to the last
by a slender steel pin. history, that grim curatorial
shuffle. infinity of sifted bone. syntax, context,
liars, and spiders. most articulate emergency,

history. what is mimicked. what is cloned. 'merica.
doing porajmos two, electric boogaloo. doing
the museum as theme park. funding genocide
by william castle. *angerlund* is a child's tongue
punished at a ribbon cutting. malignant
deliverance, flagon of mead. we're lost.
in unemployment's algorithm, opioids
and glycerines. the water rising, morphing
north. how skies are purged of birds.
how motorcades and unconcern. so
many screens, so many eyes, surfeit, debased.
desire lies only in the ear, or the frontier of our
fingertips. and by desire, some dreamier eternal.
a word might matter waking maybe recognize
a friend.

Notes on the Poems

When **R&C** (see what I did, there?) was first published, finding someone willing to write an intro proved impossible. I am still not entirely surprised. Respectable Christian Communist scholars were perhaps naturally reticent to lend their names to a series of poems featuring, among other dubious delights, the grim spectacle of Soho renting, paeans to unshaved pubic hair; drug abuse, Donald Trump, Joy Division, and paedophile decapitation. A friend of mine distilled this reluctance quite succinctly: *Umm [pregnant pause], I'm really not sure about this one, Fran.*

I get it. I do. For those with faith the poems' mix of lavish lyric style and grimy violence might appear to approach their materials with an inappropriate ribaldry, ambivalence or scepticism. For those without faith, who insist on the mutual exclusivity of radical politics and spiritual belief, the book is a kind of embarrassing paradox, an inelegant attempt to reconcile two conflicting modes of thought. Having my cake and eating it too.

But I'm not that fond of cake, to be honest. This book grew out of a profound, lifelong engagement with liberation theology, the radical notion that God, as presented in scripture, rides on the side of the marginalised and the oppressed. This comes across most militantly, I think, in Luke, and in the Psalms. But it is also woven through various hagiographies, through the purported histories, writing, and examples of the saints. Saints' lives are astonishing, full of human fallibility; exemplary courage and compassion. It is in this spirit that the poems invoke and evoke them. Saintly intercession extends to us a space of radical reciprocity; the chance to be heard, to be held, by a human listener capable of empathy, who is also a spiritual actor, tireless on our behalf. Saints inspire, and they encourage. They offer us a vivid, mutually responsible socialist community. They provide us with personal succour, but they also unite and mobilize us toward collective political action in the service of those who suffer alongside us.

And who needs that more than the abused, the oppressed, the poor, the addicted, the desperately unhappy? If the book abounds in violence, angst and modern grot, then that's where we are as a society. If the speakers are fallible, ambivalent, wracked with doubt, then that's who we are as people. There's love here too. There's anger, kindness, hope. In places, there's a saint's-eye view of those we might otherwise see through the lens of pity or contempt.

There's a rich imaginative legacy in the lives of saints; a fervent polychromatic iconography. There's poetry and cunning, there's sacrifice and resistance. These poems deliberately draw from multiple Christian traditions; Greek Orthodox, German Protestant, Irish Catholic. Some of the tales are apocryphal, long since dismissed by scholars. This is deliberate: this isn't a book about what I believe, it's about the wealth of radical inspiration to be drawn from spiritual sources. It's about the stories people have made from their oppression, and the figures whose examples have kept them strong. You don't have to believe to read this book, and this isn't an evangelical exercise. It is a book about the need for such stories, such examples; their wonderfully invigorating and subversive potential.

+

'**In need of saints**': I've always been bothered by a consensus on the liberal Left that religion is a con, practiced against the ignorant, in the service of mass exploitation. I've been bothered because this consensus doesn't trouble to distinguish between the worst excesses of organised religion and sustaining acts of personal faith. Rather, there's a sneering or a snobbery directed toward those who believe, an accusation of moral abdication, cowardice and woolly-thinking. I've been bothered because this kind of criticism is generally emanating from sedentary, intellectual enclaves, and not, say, from inside of occupied territories, fascistic regimes, demilitarised zones, refugee camps, tent cities, halting sites or slums.

In the poem, the impetus toward prayer grows out of intolerable conditions of poverty and abuse. The speaker addresses the saints because her bruised and battered faith will no longer allow for a merciful, all-powerful God, and her sense of shame requires a human listener. Prayer is one of the very few places the speaker can go to experience a sense of community with women and girls who suffer like herself. I very much see the strength she draws from these moments of communion as the beginnings of a connection to the wider world, of a forging of affinities with living, breathing others. This poem recognises that an imaginative solidarity is often the only solidarity on offer, but also knows that an imaginative solidarity can be the beginning of great things.

'**Justina**': Saint Justina of Padua, a virgin of noble birth, who pledged herself to perpetual virginity and the teachings of Christ from an early age. According to legend she was martyred in 303 AD after refusing the advances of the Roman Emperor Maximian. My starting point for this poem was Justina's suggestive and confusing iconography. She is often depicted with a unicorn, and holding a sword to her breast. Both these symbols figure for a vulnerable, yet fiercely guarded virginity. She is also frequently pictured with a book, and as a nun. Justina never was a nun, but the poem supposes she desperately wanted to be one, and it turns the bleak carceral vision of the convent on its head, making it a place of refuge and potential sorority for a young woman wishing to avoid the snares of marriage and the oppressive expectations of femininity. The poem is a kind of sleight. On first reading it might appear she's running *from* convent life, but in actual fact the cloister walls offer her a scene of daring escape. I wanted to reinvest the image of an impossibly perfect virgin martyr with vivacity and flare. To set her brave refusal to submit in a human context, making her a model of not merely virtuous sacrifice but integrity and self-determination.

'**Sebastian in Soho**': Saint Sebastian was an early Christian martyr, put to death during the reign of Diocletian, when a persecutory mania against the Christian sect was sweeping Rome. Initially he was tied to a tree, or possibly a post, and riddled with arrows. This did not kill him (in some versions of the legend he was rescued by Saint Irene of Rome), but upon his recovery he went to Diocletian to warn him of his sins. Diocletian had him clubbed to death, and his body thrown into the common sewer. Along with the legend of his martyrdom, this poem draws together a variety of representational strands, foremost being St Sebastian's status as a protector against plague, his patronage of pin-makers, and the dying, and his uneasy position as gay icon in visual art.

The 'plague' evoked by this poem is the AIDS epidemic of the 80s and 90s, and its scene is one of substance abuse and sexual exploitation. The Sebastian of the title refers both to the poem's subject and his saintly namesake, whom I imagine narrating events with a mixture of tenderness and exasperation. Idolised and invoked by his unlikely devotee, the saint refuses to look away. He cannot provide adequate protection, but instead offers an intercession of mercy and compassion on behalf of the dying boy. The poem partakes of Saint Sebastian's troubling iconography, asking how aesthetic and sensual pleasure can exist within the borders of grievous bodily harm. There's desire here, and various kinds of longing, but these run parallel to the depiction of a central human figure in a state of gradual wreckage. It is, I think, an accusation of complacency and a call for compassion.

'**Uncumber/ Wilgefortis speaks**': The story of Uncumber is more folktale than canonical religious text, but she's persisted nonetheless, in popular imagination since the 14th century. Uncumber prayed to God that she might resist a forced marriage to an abusive husband. God answered her prayer in a somewhat unusual fashion, granting her the growth of a frankly luxurious beard as a way of circumventing male lust. In many versions of the legend, she was crucified and burnt to death by her own father as a result. I knew as soon as I saw the painting of Uncumber by Hieronymus Bosch that I was going to write this poem. I think the appearance and persistence of her cult says so much about the horrors that have historically beset women, and the double-bind in which male desire has consistently placed us. Uncumber was punished for being beautiful, forced to marry a man she despised, and she was punished for being 'ugly', martyred for her aesthetic defiance of patriarchal power. I wanted Uncumber's voice to be unapologetic and defiant. It saddens me that the only possible outcome for her legend anyone could conceive of was her murder. She incites us to look forward to a time when women's bodies (and souls) will not be up for grabs, when it is possible to live without complying or conforming. I dedicate this piece to my own radical feminist hero, and to all our militant foremothers.

'Bury the wren': Saint Stephen is venerated as the first martyr of Christianity. A deacon in the early church, Stephen was tried for blasphemy for his teachings. At his trial, he made a long speech denouncing the Jewish authorities who were sitting in judgment on him. He was summarily stoned to death. Due to the manner of his martyrdom, Saint Stephen is especially invoked for protection in times of persecution. His feast day is on the 26th of December, which in Ireland is still known as Wren's Day. The poem takes its title from a children's song sung during the Wren's Day celebrations: *The wren the wren the king of all birds / On St Stephen's Day was caught in the furze/ Up with the kettle and down with the pan/ Give us a penny for to bury the wran.* Crowds of mummers, dressed in straw suits and motley would hunt a fake wren through the village, then go house to house playing music in celebration of its capture. A kind of wake for the wren. The poem draws from both Christian and pagan traditions in an act of lamentation. This is the most personal poem in the book, a payer for deliverance from the sectarian hatreds that have riven Ireland for centuries, and that continue to afflict, unequally, the poorest and most vulnerable.

'The girl with kaleidoscope eyes': Saint Lucy of Syracuse has a fascinating, somewhat Gothic legend. She consecrated her virginity to God from an early age and pledged her dowry to the poor, but her mother, who was sick, and who feared for her daughter's future without a protector, arranged for her marriage to a man of wealthy pagan family. Lucy was a devotee of Saint Agatha, often kneeling to pray at her shrine; she persuaded her mother to make a pilgrimage there, and while her mother made that pilgrimage Lucy had a vision of Saint Agatha, who told her that because of her faith her mother would indeed be cured. When her mother regained her health Lucy persuaded her to distribute a great part of her riches among the poor. When Lucy's betrothed heard news that her patrimony and jewels were being given away, he denounced her to the Governor of Syracuse as a Christian. The Governor ordered her to burn a sacrifice to the emperor's image, and when she refused he sentenced her to be 'defiled'.

Here's where it gets really interesting: when the guards came to take her away, they could not move her even when they hitched her to a team of oxen; bundles of wood were then heaped about her and set on fire, but would not burn. She eventually met her death by sword. That Lucy had her eyes gouged out is a relatively recent (15th Century) addition to the story. In some versions she prophesied the end of Roman rule and had her eyes taken from her in punishment, in other versions she removed her own eyes to discourage a persistent suitor who admired them. The poem embraces both versions, giving the Lucy invoked by the speaker both agency and prescient power.

The feast of Saint Lucy's Day takes place on the 13th of December, during Advent. It is evoked in the Donne poem, 'A Nocturnal upon St. Lucy's Day', lines and conceits from which the poem plays with. The protagonist in this poem conflates Saint Lucy with The Beatles' 'Lucy in the Sky with Diamonds', seeing a vision of her with faceted and shining eyes within a humdrum scene of suburban suppression. Saint Lucy is invoked against temptations of the flesh and worldly desire. The poem figures these desires not as sexual but material, catalogue furniture, watered silk, colour televisions. The poem's speaker sees through these things to the hollowness and misery behind them. She prays to Saint Lucy in hope of another kind of life.

'**Radical Savant, Newbury 1994**': Saint Francis of Assisi, former 13th Century wide boy, Franciscan convert, ascetic scholar and patron saint of ecology and animals, of all the Saints has left perhaps the most compelling written legacy, radical in its message of mutual care and redistributive justice. This was the second piece I wrote for this sequence, having recently read both a life of Saint Francis, and the 2018 collection of poems by Ann Wroe. Although Wroe's poetry is beautiful, and eloquent of the saint's spiritual enlightenment, I didn't feel the frenetic throb of Francis' injunction to *vivere sine proprio* through the thread of her text; his dedication not to charity or 'alms', but justice, or the deep way in which he understood his poverty as part of the poverty of others. Whatever he had at his disposal was always connected to the question of what 'other poor people' would need. The needs of others had priority over his own, and to act otherwise would have been 'theft'.

Francis' writing isn't just a mystical exhortation to love and care for all things, but a call to radical action, a reimagining of the way we live our lives in order to transform the world. It seemed logical to me, therefore, that he'd appear within my own crusty New Age cohort, during the Newbury Bypass protests in the mid nineteen-nineties. This poem is set during the dismantling and eviction of the Tot Hill camp. It is both a poem of admiration and one of communion, connecting the writing and teachings of Francis to a long lineage of protest and dissent.

'**Our Aggie**': According to legend Agnes of Rome was condemned two times, first, to be dragged naked through the streets to a brothel, and second, to be bound to a stake and burnt to death. In the first instance tradition records that those who tried to rape her were struck blind, and in the second, that the flames parted and would not burn her. This did not save her. The officer in charge of her burning drew his sword and cut off her head. Because of her martyrdom Agnes is patron saint of those seeking chastity and purity. Agnes is also the patron saint of young girls.

Folk custom calls for them to invoke her on Saint Agnes Eve (20th January) with a view to discovering their future husbands, a superstition immortalised in John Keats's poem, 'The Eve of Saint Agnes'. Nothing so innocent takes place in this poem, which sees young women placed in the extremis of abuse: exploitation, rape, and ultimately murder. Let's face it, the annals of history are thick with the bodies of women and girls who have been murdered by sexually predatory men. And I've often felt the (not exclusively) Catholic church's response to this is muddled, venerating murdered virgin saints, and appearing to prefer girls dead than as rape survivors. It's as if a portion of the rapist's sinfulness gloms onto the victim, so that only her lack of victimhood—her intact hymen—is proof of her unsullied virtue. This poem takes liberties, then. The Aggie in this poem suffers the worst abasement imaginable, she doesn't remain intact, or pure, or inviolable, and yet she is still exemplary. It's a poem that recognises we need a better definition of 'virtue'. Something I feel the original Agnes would have understood.

'**All the errors and mistakes**': It is Chaucer's *Parliament of Fowls* that contains the first extant reference to Saint Valentine's Day as an occasion for romance. The tradition probably existed before this, but Chaucer is our main surviving source of the Saint's connection with love and with lovers. Valentine was originally the patron saint of epilepsy, invoked against headaches and fainting and plague. Valentine is a slippery character, and it's difficult to definitively pin down or tease apart his legend. Common hagiography describes Saint Valentine as a priest of Rome, put to death by the emperor Claudius Gothicus for his evangelism. He was said to have been beaten by clubs and beheaded when he would not renounce his faith.

The apocryphal folkloric elements of his story fascinated me, before he was put to death, Valentine was said to have sent a note to the daughter of his jailer, whom he had healed. The note was signed 'Your Valentine', and according to tradition this is where the practice of giving cards, or notes on Valentine's Day originated. Another superstition of Saint Valentine has him secretly performing marriage ceremonies for Christian couples, allowing the husbands involved to avoid conscription into the Roman army. To remind these husbands of their vows and God's love, Valentine was said to have given them hearts cut from parchment. This portion of the legend is highly spurious. For this poem I merge Saint Valentine's complicated legend with the complex, highly apocryphal legend of Joy Division's Ian Curtis, himself an epileptic, whose dominant myth has him die for love, or for some romantic notion of unassuageable melancholia. This poem is really about a desire for human connection beyond the mediating muddle of our myths; how our stories and our lives become twisted over time. I imagine a connection between the petitioner and the Saint that cuts through all that bullshit static, that makes both subjects new and whole.

'Rita of the White Bees': Anyone who knows me even slightly well will know I have a special place in my heart for Saint Rita of Cascia, who is patron of abused women, hopeless causes, infertility, illness, mothers and widows. She is invoked especially against loneliness and against domestic violence. Rita was born in 1381 and given in an arranged marriage at the age of twelve to a violent husband. She endured his abuse, both physical and mental for many years, and, according to popular tales, was able through forbearance, kindness and compassion, to convert her husband to a better life. Not that this availed him much. He was stabbed to death by a member of a rival family.

One of the least palatable elements of Rita's legend is that rather than have her two sons commit the mortal sin of murder by pledging *La Vendetta* against their father's killer, she prayed that God would take them. They died of dysentery a year later. Rita had wanted, her entire life, to join the convent of Saint Magdalene, but could not do so until the age of thirty-six. The nuns at Saint Magdalene recognised her piety, but were afraid of being associated with the long-running blood feud in which Rita found herself embroiled. In order that she might finally join the convent, Rita set about reconciling and establishing peace between the rival families of Cascia. Tradition records that, this accomplished, Rita was transported into the garden courtyard of Saint Magdalene at night. By levitation. Most of the depictions of Rita show her with the divine stigmata she received to her forehead at the age of sixty, but the title of the poem alludes to her early life, and a tradition that attends her christening, when a swarm of white bees was seen to be flying around her as she slept in her crib, peacefully entering and exiting her mouth. This uncanny event was considered an early indicator of sainthood, and for me, it presages Rita's difficult, unenviable position as a life-long mediator and peacemaker. This is a position in which many women find themselves, and Rita's veneration is particularly strong in Ireland, especially within Traveller communities, where women negotiate with skill the unstable and often violent world of men, a world where they're driven to desperate choices. What I love about the picture is that it gives Rita back her childhood: a twelve-year-old Rita in the convent garden, full of joy and life. The poem is a prayer from the lost childhoods and used up youths of other women and girls, those for whom escape is not possible.

'**Saint Martin in Euston**': Saint Martin of Tours is another Saint in whom I have a special personal interest. Patron of beggars, recovering alcoholics, horses and equestrians, and invoked especially against poverty and homelessness, the poem sees Saint Martin transported to the Euston Road, where I work most days, and where the number of people sleeping rough has recently reached an all-time high. The legend and iconography of Saint Martin has him cut his military cloak in two to clothe a beggar at the gates of the city of Amiens. That night Martin dreamt of Jesus, wearing the half-cloak he had given away. In some versions of the story, when Martin awoke, the cloak was once again made whole.

Martin's hagiography is full of surprising and uncanny incidents: Martin raising the dead, Martin turning a raging fire back from a house, Martin casting out devils, but it is this story, I think, one of exemplary and instinctive kindness, that is the most impressive of all. It isn't the miraculous incidents of Martin's life that make him venerable, and worthy of our respect, it's the very human act of responding to someone in need. And it's an act that has become increasingly rare. Partly, this is complacency, but more than that, I think it's a sense of being overwhelmed. The scale of the problem is so vast, we simply stop seeing it. We don't recognise homeless people, only the amorphous blight of homelessness, a thing we are individually powerless to do anything about. And I think we feel guilty for that, and so we rationalise our inertia with epithets about how 'they'll only spend the money on drugs / alcohol', etc. Martin leads the charge in this poem in an act of radical remembrance and recognition. On behalf of those who suffer, and on behalf of all those who have lost people to homelessness, and the associated horrors of alcoholism and substance abuse, it is a plea to see the person behind the problem, and an acknowledgement that each individual act of kindness is accretive and contributive to a change that's bound to come.

'And Margaret is swallowed by Satan in the shape of a dragon': At the time of writing the number of people who have died after being declared 'fit to work' by the Department for Work and Pensions stands at ninety people per month. I make no bones about it, this is a poem viscerally angry about the consequences of Tory economic policy and the bastards who administer it. Margaret of Antioch is patron of peasants, exiles, falsely accused people, and the dying. This seems apt to me. Although the version of Margaret's hagiography as appears in the *Golden Legend* has her tortured by Olybrius, Governor of Rome, for her refusal of his proposal, it discounts the more miraculous incidents that take place during her torture, most significantly Margaret's being swallowed by Satan in the shape of a dragon. This aspect of her torture, however, was popularly depicted during the Middle Ages, and I think that says something about the way in which people experienced their subjection to authority. It didn't seem out of place that such an exaggerated or dramatic torture would form part of the machinery of (in)justice. People in the Middle Ages were not stupid, so it seems likely enough that, although not understood literally, the legend offers a highly vivid metaphor for individual lives swallowed up by great cruelty and iniquity. The same seems true today, so here is Margaret swallowed by a very different dragon, tortured in a far more subtle, but equally vindictive way. Now considered to be largely apocryphal, Margaret is reincarnated here, because we are more in need than ever of miraculous escapes. And Margaret does escape. Swallowed by the beast her crucifix irritates his innards, and she is spewed out.

'Homobonus in Primark': Homobonus is an unusual one. His life and beliefs seem to inaugurate the notion of a welfare state. This twelfth century merchant believed that God had allowed him to work in order that he might support those living in a state of poverty. He is patron of businesspeople, clothworkers and tailors, and his reputation is one of scrupulous honesty, donating a large proportion of his profits to the relief of the poor, and never exploiting the labour of others. This saint has had something of a strange afterlife, his likeness now being sold as a novelty item to executive types in the USA.

This seems like missing the point somewhat. The poem transplants Homobonus from his native Cremona to Primark on the Tottenham Court Road, grotesque scene of ethical abandonment if ever there was one. Primark have still not adequately addressed their use of sweatshop labour. In 2013 one of their factories in Dhaka collapsed killing and trapping hundreds of workers. At a subsequent demonstration in Dhaka in 2015 grieving protestors were met with violence by police. Primark avoided paying over 9 billion in corporation tax last year, FYI. But whenever I mention the above, I am typically treated to a reactionary blather about Primark's 'reforms'. Bollocks. 'Reforms' are the emergency manoeuvres of any chronically compromised system.

Primark might have signed up to the Ethical Trading Initiative, but the ETI is largely toothless, and still doesn't guarantee workers the payment of a living wage. Further, Primark outsource manufacturing to their suppliers which effectively means that for all their big talk about vetting factories and auditing they do not control their supply chain, allowing them to effectively shirk responsibility for any labour issues that take place there. Their whole business model is shitty: cheap, poorly made clothes at great cost to the environment and to garment workers. And who has to shop here? Other poor people, because there's precious little alternative. The poem tries to imagine what Homobonus would make of all this, as both an ethical exemplar for good business practice, and as a lover of beautiful, well-made clothes. There's great sadness and bewilderment in this poem, only some of which is my own.

'**Enter Judith (Jael, Deborah)**': Judith is less a saint than an epic hero, but in the mediaeval world she was especially venerated. 'The Book of Judith' is included in the Catholic Old Testament but excluded and consigned to the apocrypha by Protestants. Only the Coptic Church celebrates her memory in the Calendar of Saints. What interested me about her legend was its numerous resurgences throughout history. During these moments, Judith seems to figure allegorically for an oppressed but righteous people confronting, and ultimately prevailing, over the superior might of a seemingly unbeatable enemy. In 'The Book of Judith', Judith decapitates the Assyrian general Holofernes, a feat she is able to accomplish due to his great lust for her.

Scholars have frequently compared Judith to the Jael or 'Yael' sequence in the Hebrew Bible. Jael drives a tent peg through the skull of Sisera, an enemy Canaanite general and (according to some readings of the text) her would-be rapist. Deborah, the only female judge to be named in the Bible, prophesied the Israelites' victory over Sisera at the hands of a woman, and the three are often considered together by feminist scholars, concerned with moments of female agency and self-determination within Biblical texts. The speaker in this poem is both a modern reworking of Judith, and also her petitioner in the medieval mould, as she prepares for righteous battle against a superior enemy. There was a bit of a you-can't-write-that moment when I first started kicking around the idea for this poem. I'd been studying the Old English poem 'Judith' with my students, and it seemed to me it spoke to a contemporary need for a heroic triumph over monstrous men and their monstrous predations. I see this poem as a counterpart to '**Our Aggie**'; this is girlhood in unladylike resurgence against those who would exploit, suppress and silence us. It is a cathartic allegory for a world in which just staying alive is sometimes the biggest victory we can claim.

'**Anthony After All**': Anthony of Padua, invoked to find lost things, patron of lost people, poor people, lost souls, runts of the litter, amputees, mariners and travellers. Famed for his eloquence, Anthony is often pictured with an open book and a flaming heart. In the legend of his life Anthony had a book of psalms stolen from him; when he prayed for its return it was brought back by the repentant thief. He died of ergotamine poisoning, and his legend states that when he died, bells rung spontaneously. Tony (Anthony) Hancock, was a British comedian who committed suicide in June 1968, overdosing on barbitone and alcohol. The *Hancock's Half Hour* episode entitled 'The Missing Page' features the eponymous protagonist trying desperately to recover the end of the fictional noir thriller, *Lady Don't Fall Backwards*. This last is now also the title of a song by Pete Doherty.

This poem brings these various elements together somewhat whimsically, attempting to capture Hancock's characteristic idiom and cadence in what is less an invocation of the saint, than an offer of comfort extended by him. The figures that populate and are threaded through this poem are all, in one way or another, 'lost souls' to whom Saint Anthony extends his comfort and his empathy.

'**Rollox and his dog**': Saint Roch (known also as Saint Rollox in Scotland, said to be a corruption of Saint Roch's Loch near Glasgow) is patron of dogs, falsely accused people, invalids and pilgrims. He is especially invoked against epidemics and diseases. According to his legend, on the death of his parents he distributed all his worldly goods among the poor and set out for Rome as a mendicant pilgrim. Arriving in Italy during a virulent epidemic of plague, he began tending to the sick with great zeal until he himself became ill and was expelled from the town. He withdrew into the nearby forest where a dog is said to have supplied him with bread and licked his wounds. That animal saved the Saint's life. It is this episode of Roch's legend that the poem draws on.

Contemplating the story, I'm struck especially by the way Roch was expelled by society when he became sick, after diligently ministering to those with plague. I've been thinking about this a lot lately, the great injustice by which the poor are tolerated only as long as they are healthy and useful; the way in which we, as a society, do not extend care to those who become sick or incapable in mind or in body, especially if the symptoms of that sickness are uncouth or unappealing. Animals do not make such distinctions. The relationships forged between homeless humans and their dogs is a powerful and moving testament to this. Animal relationships often offer us an ideal model of mutual care, one we find difficult to sustain with other people. The Rollox of this poem knows this. His is not a petition for human compassion but a prayer of gratitude for canine kindness received. In my other life as a dog-whisperer I've often wished people were more like pit-bulls. I still think that now. They put us to shame.

'**Bernie**': Saint Bernadette, Bernadette Soubirous, was a poor girl known for her humility and devotion to her faith, whose Marian visions were responsible for the founding of the Sanctuary of Our Lady of Lourdes. She is patron of those ridiculed for their faith and is especially invoked against poverty. Due to contracting cholera as a child, she was sickly for most of her life, and a slow learner who could read and write very little. At the time of her visions her family were living in such an extreme of poverty that they occupied one single basement room, formerly used as a jail, known locally as *le cachot*, 'the dungeon'. Bernadette experienced her first vision at the age of fourteen when collecting firewood with her sister. A 'dazzling light, and a white figure' appeared to her in a grotto. She returned to the spot the following Sunday after Mass, and again saw the apparition, which asked her to return to the grotto every day for a fortnight. This she did.

Her visions divided the town in which she lived, some believed her, while others demanded she be sent to an asylum. Many who interviewed her found her simple-minded, but the church authorities who investigated her visions in 1862 confirmed the authenticity of her apparitions, causing a chapel to be built on the site of the grotto. The Sanctuary of Our Lady of Lourdes is now one of the world's major Catholic pilgrimage sites.

What prompted this poem was the idea that faith could be both an avenue of imaginative escape and a source of power for those without any other options. Bernadette Soubrious, a semi-literate girl living in poverty nevertheless shaped the future and fortunes of the Catholic church through her Marian visions, visions which others considered symptomatic of madness. The Bernie of the poem also has visions, visions that are quickly discounted, ridiculed and despised both by her peers and by the authority figures in her life who demand that faith conform to one predetermined, clearly defined shape. This poem is a petition against ridicule, and a celebration of the imagination. It is for the rich, strange landscapes of the mind, and our right to believe in our own way.

'**Imbolc**': This poem celebrates and invokes Brigid of Kildare, who is said to be a Christianisation of the Goddess Bríg, one of the Tuatha Dé Danann, Goddess of corn, fertility, and spring. The rituals mentioned in the poem are those practiced in rural Ireland and Scotland, conflating and merging pagan and Christian traditions of Brigid. In Catholicism, Brigid is patron saint of children whose parents are not married, children with abusive fathers, children born of abusive unions, poets, scholars and travellers. She has a very special place in my heart. I think my very first exposure to Saint Brigid was the painting by John Duncan, where she's born aloft by angels in fabulously patchworked robes, so she's always been associated with magic for me. I also love the traditions of her miracles, which seem both wily and slightly fierce, for example, there's the legend of her cloak, which grew in all directions to cover acres and acres of land, having once asked the parsimonious King of Leinster for as much land as her cloak would cover.

And then there is the legend of her eyes, where Brigid's brothers, annoyed by her dedication to God and the subsequent loss of her bride price tried to marry her off to a man named Bacene whether she liked it or not. Bacene told Brigid that her beautiful eye would be his, and in response she thrust her finger in her own eye, saying she thought it unlikely anyone would pay for a blind girl. Oh, and she also told Bacene that his two eyes would explode in his head. Which they promptly did. The poem tries to recreate that childhood sense of uncanniness surrounding Brigid's legends, and the private rituals children build around their own stories.

'**Lamplighters**': The communion of saints is a kind of spiritual union in which all members of the Christian church, living and dead, are joined. Each member forms part of a single 'mystical body', individually contributing to the good of all, mutually responsible for the welfare of all. Whether you believe in Saints or not, it's not a massive imaginative leap from the communion of saints to the communism of people. This poem broaches the idea that regardless of faith, we *are* connected, that we do belong to a long historical continuum of solidarity. From this we may take comfort and be inspired to fight for one another.

'**Prayers and Maledictions**': My starting point for these poems were the 'terrible sonnets' of Gerard Manley Hopkins, by way of Psalm 88. Hopkins describes a feeling of being 'pitched past pitch of grief', where the voice of Psalm 88 speaks woundedly of feeling 'like those who have no help, like those forsaken among the dead'. Unlike the majority of the lament Psalms, Psalm 88 does not resolve itself in praise. It is loss and misery without remedy; it is exile, absence and diminishment, materially, bodily, socially and emotionally. So my impetus was in poems of desperation, and lyric abjection which might seem like an odd choice for a book themed around miraculous experience, but this is another kind of prayer—prayer as testimony, prayer as witnessing; prayer as place protest and ethical questioning. It is an agonised railing against all that besets us, one that attempts to negotiate between the pain felt by an individual and the collective radical engagement such an individual demands.

These aren't poems of personal catharsis; they're rebarbative linguistic experiences, intended to retune, attune and unify us together towards radical action. Or that's the idea anyway. The poems may fall short, but I believe in the attempt.

Note on the author

Fran Lock is the author of numerous chapbooks and fourteen poetry collections, most recently *Hyena!* (Poetry Bus Press, 2023), shortlisted for the T.S. Eliot Prize 2023, *'a disgusting lie': further adventures through the neo-liberal hell-mouth* (Pamenar Press, 2023), and *The New Herbal* (Blueprint Press, 2024). Fran was the Judith E. Wilson Poetry Fellow at Cambridge University (2022-23), researching feral subjectivity through the lens of the medieval Bestiary. *Vulgar Errors/ Feral Subjects*, a collection of essays based on her work at Cambridge, was published by Out-Spoken Press last year. Fran is a Commissioning Editor for radical arts and culture cooperative **Culture Matters**, and she edits the Soul Food column for *Communist Review*.

By the same author

Poetry Collections as author:

The New Herbal
(Blueprint Press, 2024)

'a disgusting lie' (further adventures through the neoliberal hell mouth)
(Pamenar Press, 2023)

Hyena!
(Poetry Bus Press, 2023)

White/ Other
(87 Press, 2022)

Forever Alive
(Dare-Gale Press, 2022)

Hyena! Jackal! Dog!
(Pamenar Press, 2021)

Contains Mild Peril
(Out Spoken Press, 2019)

Raptures and Captures
(Culture Matters, 2019)

Triptych
(with Korliss Sewer and Fióna Bolger)
(Poetry Bus Press, 2019)

Co-Incidental 1
(Black Light Engine Room Press, 2018)

Ruses and Fuses
(Culture Matters, 2018)

Dogtooth
(Out Spoken Press, 2017)

Laudanum Chapbook Anthology: Volume Two
(Laudanum, 2017)

Muses and Bruises
(Culture Matters, 2017)

The Mystic and the Pig Thief
(Salt, 2014)

Flatrock
(Little Episodes, 2011)

As Editor

A Brief and Biased History of Love, Alan Humm
(Culture Matters, 2023)

The Haunting: Deleted Scenes, Kevin Patrick McCann
(Culture Matters, 2023)

Machine/ Language, Martin Hayes
(Culture Matters, 2023)

Rebel Admin, Al Hutchins
(Culture Matters, 2023)

The Cry of the Poor: An anthology of radical writing about poverty
(Culture Matters, 2021)

Witches, Warriors, Workers: An anthology of contemporary working women's poetry (with Jane Burn)
(Culture Matters, 2020)

As Translator

Leaving by Anar (assisting Hari Rajaledchumy)
(Poetry Translation Centre, 2021)

Creative Non-fiction

Vulgar Errors/ Feral Subjects
(Out-Spoken Press, 2023)

Forthcoming

*Love is Stronger than Death:
Mary Magdalene and the Insurrection of Jesus*
(Culture Matters, 2025)

BV - #0147 - 070725 - C6 - 210/148/9 - PB - 9781912710768 - Matt Lamination